STANDARD HISTORY

People and Power: Germany

1918-1939

Ian Matheson

Hodder & Stoughton
LONDON SYDNEY AUCKLAND

Acknowledgements

The author would like to thank Bill Hannah of Kilmarnock for help in finding sources B and C in chapter 12 and Mrs Theresa Keith of Dumbarton for permission to use source C in chapter 17.

The Publishers would like to thank the following for permission to reproduce copyright illustrations: The Illustrated London News Picture Library p6. The Weimar Archive p7; p8; p13; p19; p26; p29; p30; p33; p35 top; p39; p41 top; p43; p44; p45; p50; p52; p58; p59; p62; p66; p70; p73. Ullstein Bilderdienst p9; p23. Hulton-Deutsch Collection/The Hulton Picture Company cover; p10; p11; p37; p38; p48; p63. 'The Signing of the Peace in the Hall of Mirrors, Versailles', 1919 by Sir William Orpen by permission of The Imperial War Museum, London p14. The Imperial War Museum Photographic Collection p27; p61 both; p53 right. John Heartfield p45; p57; p65. Punch Publications p18. Popperfoto p25; p34; p68. Topham p31; p42; p64 right; p74 left. Suddeutscher-Verlag p35 bottom; p40; p56; p64 left. Camera Press p41 bottom. Institute of Contemporary History & Weiner Library p49. David Low, Evening Standard/Centre for the Study of Cartoon and Caricature, University of Kent at Canterbury p55; p77. Archiv Gerstenberg p74 right.

The Publishers would also like to thank the following for permission to reproduce material in this volume: Andre Deutsch Ltd for the extract from *A Boy in Your Situation* by Charles Hannam; Chatto & Windus for the extract from *The Naked Years: Growing up in Nazi Germany* by Marianne Mackinnon; © Christabel Bielenberg 1970. Extracted *The Past is Myself* published by Corgi. All rights reserved; Edward Arnold for the extract from *A History of Germany 1815-1945* by William Carr; the extract from *Nazi Propaganda* by Z A B Zeman (2nd edition, 1973) reproduced by permission of Oxford University Press; Peters Fraser & Dunlop for the extract from *The Age of Upheaval* by J M Roberts.

Every effort has been made to trace and acknowledge ownership of copyright. The publishers will be glad to make suitable arrangements with any copyright holders whom it has not been possible to contact.

British Library Cataloguing in Publication Data

Matheson, Ian
People and power: Germany 1918-1939.
– (Standard grade history)
I. Title II. Series
943.085

ISBN 0-340-54213-6

First published 1992

Typeset by Litho Link Ltd, Welshpool, Powys, Wales.
Printed in Great Britain for the educational publishing division of Hodder & Stoughton Ltd, Mill Road, Dunton Green, Sevenoaks, Kent by Thomson Litho, East Kilbride.

CONTENTS

SERIES PREFACE

The books in this series are designed to present major historical themes, change, co-operation and conflict, people and power. Key ideas in British, European and World history derived from these themes provide the basis for the organisation of content. The books make use of different types of evidence – primary and secondary, written, statistical and pictorial. Users of the books are guided towards their own understanding of history, based on their individual abilities and interests, as each section (chapter) progresses from simpler statements of ideas and issues to a consideration and analysis of more detailed and complex evidence.

It is the hope of the authors that the books in the series will increase understanding of the chosen themes as well as enthusiasm for investigating people, actions and events in history. Those who use the books will be encouraged to decide for themselves about the evidence they contain and to have their own views of the past.

Graeme Coy.

1 THE END OF THE REICH

Defeat for the Army

1918 was a bad year in which to be a German. True, it started well enough. In March, the war in the east came to an end when the new Communist government in Russia signed the Treaty of Brest-Litovsk. Suddenly, Germany had a million extra soldiers to fight in the west.

General Ludendorff's new storm troops broke out of the trenches that had held the armies for almost four years. They drove the British and French back so quickly that it seemed they might take Paris. Germany might win the war before American reinforcements could help the Allies. Then, just as had happened in 1914, they were stopped and turned back at the river Marne.

Ludendorff called 8 August 1918, 'the Black Day of the German Army'. On that day the Allies began their attack, the soldiers supported by 3,400 big guns and 600 tanks. For the next two months they pushed the Germans back towards the Rhine. German soldiers lost heart.

A I was told of behaviour which I should not have thought possible in the German Army; whole bodies of our men had surrendered to single troopers. Retiring troops, meeting a fresh division going bravely into action, had shouted out things like "Blackleg" and "You're prolonging the war".

Ludendorff, My War Memoirs.

The soldiers of the countries allied to Germany were also tired of the war. In September and October 1918 Germany's allies Bulgaria, Turkey and Austria surrendered.

By early October the generals, Ludendorff and Hindenburg, knew that the war was lost. They decided to ask the Allies to stop fighting.

The suffering of the people

Throughout the war the German people had suffered greatly. German food production fell badly because many farm workers had to join the army. The British navy blockaded Germany, stopping goods from reaching port. By 1918 everything – food, clothing, fuel – was in short supply. Workers went on strike to support their demand for

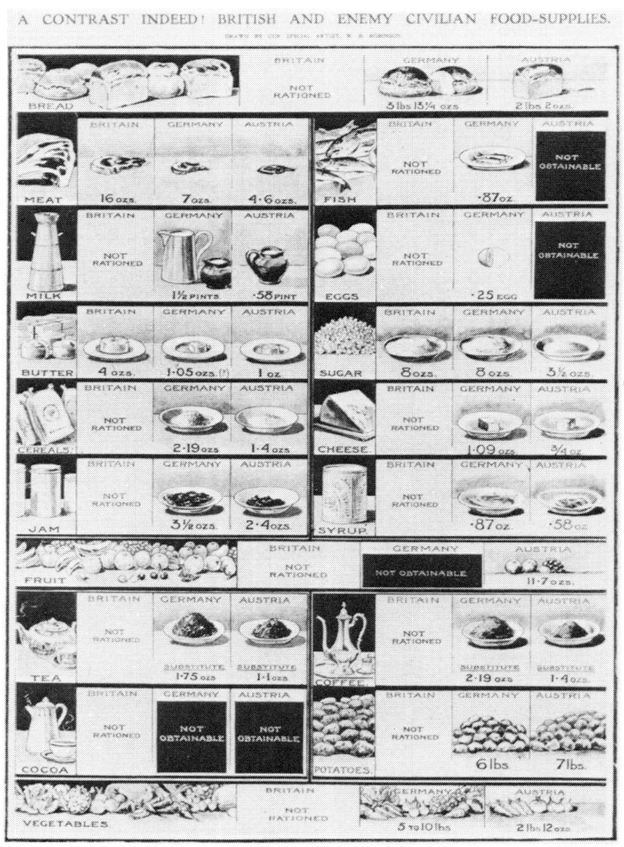

B Illustrated London News, March 1918.

C People scavenge for food on a potato field.

shorter working hours. They did this because they found it hard to work with so little to eat.

To make things even worse, a virus called Spanish 'flu hit Germany. Over 400,000 people died from this and from food shortages before the end of the year. Ordinary Germans became desperate. Many of them simply wanted the war to end. Many of them no longer trusted their country's leaders.

?

1 Copy this paragraph into your notebook, filling in the blanks. 1918 started well for ________ . ________ fell out of the war, so ________ had a ________ more soldiers to fight in the ____ . When they attacked there, the ________ advanced almost to ________ before being stopped at the river ________ .

2 Why did Ludendorff call 8 August 1918 'the Black Day of the German Army'?

3 'German soldiers lost heart.' Find two pieces of evidence in source A which support this statement.

4 Use the information in sources B and C to describe ways in which the British naval blockade made German people suffer.

5 Why, by October 1918, did many Germans want the war to end? Give as many reasons as you can.

6 Source B was published in Britain in March 1918.
a) What do you think it was trying to show its British readers?
b) Why might it not be reliable as evidence about food supplies in Germany?

THE FALL OF THE KAISER

Kaiser Wilhelm II and the generals had led Germany through the war. Now that it was lost, the army leaders did not want to be the ones to make peace. This was because –

- They did not want to accept the blame for losing the war.
- A civilian government might get a better deal from the Allies.
- They wanted to save the army's reputation, so that it would still be important after the war.
- They hoped a civilian government might help the Kaiser to keep his throne.

On 3 October Prince Max of Baden became Chancellor. He was shocked to find out how near Germany was to defeat, as the generals had kept this secret. He asked the Allies for an armistice. President Wilson of the U.S.A. insisted that the Kaiser would have to give up his throne first. Otherwise, the Allies would invade Germany. This demand was made because the Allies blamed the Kaiser personally for the death and destruction of the war. They would not deal with him.

There were problems inside Germany as well. On 29 October sailors at Kiel and Wilhelmshaven were ordered to sea for a last, desperate attack on the British navy. They refused. Although the soldiers in the army remained loyal, the naval rebellion was followed by risings all over Germany. Workers' and Soldiers' Councils were set up to run local

D Germany's military leaders, Ludendorff (right) and Hindenburg (left) discussing the war with the Kaiser (middle).

government. It looked as if Germany might have a Communist revolution like the one in Russia in 1917.

E Sailors taking part in the mutiny.

The threats from both outside and inside Germany made the government decide there was only one way out. On 6 November Friedrich Ebert, leader of the Social Democratic Party (SPD), spoke to army leaders.

F The people were widely convinced that the Kaiser was the guilty one . . . The main thing was that the people wanted to see the man they held responsible for the disaster removed from his post . . . The abdication of the Kaiser was absolutely necessary . . . to prevent revolution.

Colonel Hans von Haeften, reporting Ebert's speech.

Three days later huge crowds marched on the government buildings in Berlin. Prince Max announced that the Kaiser had abdicated. At the same time the Prince resigned to let Ebert become Chancellor. Later that day, Kaiser Wilhelm fled to Holland. The monarchy was finished, Germany had become a republic.

Within two days the armistice was signed, and the fighting came to an end. For Ebert, the problem now was to keep control in Germany. This would not be easy.

?

1. Here are some reasons why the army generals gave up power to civilians. Choose the ones you think are true and copy them into your note book.
   - They still hoped to fight on and win the war.
   - They knew the Allies would not agree to a cease-fire with them.
   - They thought they might be shot as war criminals.
   - They hoped a civilian government might save the Kaiser's throne.
   - They wanted to make civilians take the blame for losing the war.
2. Look at source E.
   a) What do you think the sailors were doing? Give a reason for your answer.
   b) The sailors had already gained some control in the city. What evidence in the picture supports this statement?
3. Explain why the Kaiser lost his throne. You should mention events inside and outside Germany in your answer.
4. a) In source F, what reason did Ebert give the army leaders why the Kaiser had to abdicate?
   b) What did Ebert think would happen if the Kaiser stayed?

2 OPPOSITION TO THE NEW REPUBLIC

The Spartacist Revolt

Ebert found himself at the head of a country in chaos. Many towns and cities were ruled by Workers' or Soldiers' Councils. Some of these just wanted to keep the peace and support law and order. Others wanted revolution to go much further. They wanted the government to break the power of the army. They also wanted it to take over industry and land, and run them for the people. This is called Socialism.

Ebert was a Socialist as well, but he wanted these things to come about gradually, by people voting for them. Those who wanted them to happen quickly, through violent revolution, were called Communists, or 'Reds'. Already, they had taken over some cities.

A 5 p.m.: Halle and Leipzig Red. Evening: Düsseldorf, Halstein, Osnabrück, Lauenburg Red; Magdeburg, Stuttgart, Oldenburg, Brunswick and Cologne all Red.

Ministry of War Report, 8 November 1918.

Ebert needed help. On 9 November he agreed with General Groener that the army would support the new government. In return, the government would fight against Communism.

The Communists were angry that Ebert's government did not follow Socialist policies. They accused him of betraying the working classes. On 6 January 1919 a band of Communists calling themselves the Spartacus League, led by Karl Liebknecht and Rosa Luxemburg, rose in Berlin. These were the Spartacists. They called a general strike. They took over important buildings, including newspaper offices, railway stations and even a brewery. They put up barriers in some of the main streets.

B Spartacists guard a street in Berlin.

● *The Freikorps*

The government needed more help than the army could give. There were others they could turn to.

Some men who had been officers in the army were left with no jobs when the army was reduced in size. They hated what had been done to Germany and to the army. They also detested Communism. These men began to form small volunteer groups called *Freikorps* (Free Corps), with some help from the government. They gathered uniforms and weapons, including field guns, machine guns and even armoured cars.

Gustav Noske, the Defence Minister, raised an army from these *Freikorps* to march on Berlin. On 11 January he led them into the centre of the city himself. They began by using artillery to capture the police headquarters from the rebels.

C *Freikorps* soldiers in Berlin.

Over the next four days the *Freikorps* defeated the rebels and took control of the city. Then they hunted down the leaders. Liebknecht and Luxemburg were arrested, and murdered the same night by *Freikorps* officers. The revolt was over, but many working-class people never forgave the government for putting it down.

?

1. Germany had become a republic. What other changes did some Socialists want it to make?
2. What did Ebert and the Communists
   a) agree about?
   b) disagree about?
3. a) What evidence is there in source A that Communists were strong in many parts of Germany?
   b) Do you think source A is a good source of information for historians? Give a reason for your answer. You might think about who wrote the source, and when it was written.
4. In sources B and C, what weapons and equipment can you see being used by
   a) the Spartacists?
   b) the Freikorps?
5. Here are some sentences. Copy them into your notebook **in the correct order** to tell the story of the Spartacist revolt in Berlin.
   – The Defence Minister led the Freikorps into the city.
   – The Spartacist leaders, Karl Leibknecht and Rosa Luxemburg, were killed.
   – The Spartacus League took over important buildings and called a general strike.
   – The government collected an army of Freikorps, volunteer groups of soldiers.
   – Within four days the rebellion collapsed.
   – The Freikorps used artillery and machine guns to defeat the rebels.

THE LEFT DIVIDED

Before 1914 the Social Democratic Party had been strong. The outbreak of war divided the Socialists: some wanted to support the war effort, but others thought that working-class people should refuse to fight each other. In 1917 they split from the majority to form the Independent Socialist Party (USPD). They were important enough, and still close enough to the SPD in their aims, for Ebert to bring them into his government. The cabinet included three members each from the SPD and the Independents.

It proved difficult for the two groups to work together. Ebert wanted to call elections to a National Assembly as soon as possible, while the Independents wanted to keep the rule of the Workers' and Soldiers' Councils. A national congress of the councils met in Berlin in December 1918. One speaker warned that a National Assembly would destroy the gains already made.

D Any clear thinking person must see that the jubilant approval of the National Assembly is equivalent to passing the death sentence on the council system . . . What is a council system to do alongside a parliamentary bourgeois democratic system? . . . In the economic sphere the old-style trade unions, aided by the National Assembly, and the middle classes will push the workers' councils out of the factories.

Speech by Ernst Daümig.

The appeal was in vain. The congress voted for an elected National Assembly.

Before elections could be held, disagreements inside the Cabinet led to the resignation of the Independents. Shortly afterwards, the Spartacists formed the German Communist Party (KPD). Now there were three groups, all claiming to represent the working class.

The Government's Reaction

Both the Independents and the Communists accused the government of making too many compromises with the old Germany: the army, the civil service and big business. They said that Ebert had betrayed the working class.

The government's reaction to the Spartacist revolt finally split the left. In fact, the rising was so badly led that it had no hope of success, as the Communists' own newspaper saw.

F Proletarians were standing shoulder to shoulder . . . They were ready to do anything, to give everything, even their lives . . .

The masses were standing from nine in the morning in the cold and fog. Somewhere their leaders were sitting and conferring. Noon came and, in addition to the cold, hunger came. And the leaders conferred . . . The fog came again and with it the dusk. The masses went home sad. They wanted great things, but they had done nothing. Because their leaders conferred.

Die Rote Fahne (The Red Flag).

Then the government called in the *Freikorps*, and used them again in Berlin and Munich later in the Spring. Their methods were often brutal. Over a thousand people, many of them innocent civilians, were killed as the risings were put down.

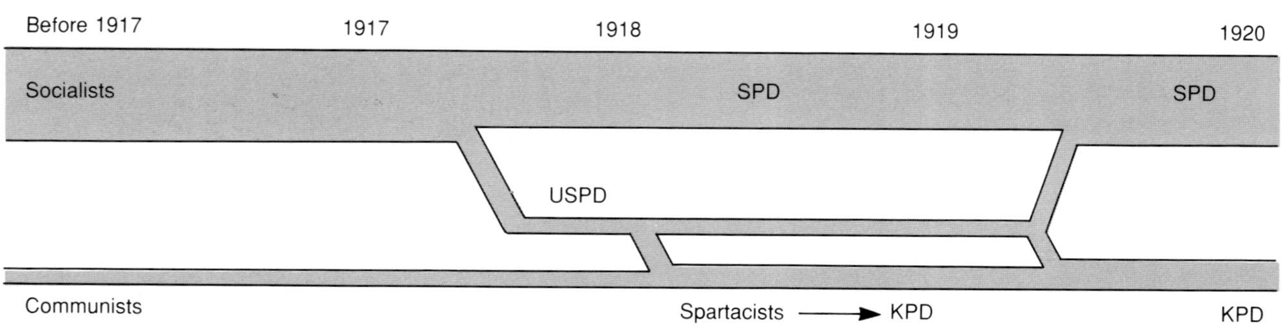

E Working-Class Groups in Germany.

G A *Freikorps* unit and armoured cars in Berlin, March 1919.

The use of these units seemed to prove that Ebert had abandoned the workers. Yet it is hard to see what else he could do if he were to avoid complete chaos. To him, Germany in 1919 needed stability more than it needed Socialism.

● *Democracy in Germany*

The long-term effects of these events were tragic for democracy in Germany. In future, the Communists detested the SPD for their actions. The two parties fought each other so hard that they divided the working-class vote at elections, and they were unable to act together against those who would become their real enemies on the right, the Nazis. In this way the German republic lost from the start one of its most important defences, the support of the class which created it.

?

1 Explain in your own words what disagreements the Independent Socialists (USPD) had with the Majority Socialists (SPD).

2 a) What political and economic reasons did Ernst Daümig give for opposition to the calling of a National Assembly? (Source D.)
b) Which party do you think Daümig supported? Give reasons for your answer.

3 What evidence is there in source F that the Spartacist rising was badly led?

4 a) What evidence is there in sources C and G that the Freikorps units were well organised and supplied?
b) What decoration has been added to the vehicles in both photographs? What does this suggest about the members of the Freikorps?

5 Write a newspaper article from a Spartacist point of view criticising the government's actions in suppressing the rising. You should suggest what attitude you expect the working class to take towards the SPD and the new republic in future. Give your article a suitable headline.

3 THE PEACE SETTLEMENT

Making the Treaty

Once the Kaiser and military government had gone, many Germans believed that the Allies no longer had a quarrel with the German people. They thought the new government would help make the peace treaty. They were wrong. They thought the treaty would be based on President Wilson's 'Fourteen Points', which had been offered to Germany as a basis for peace in 1917. They were wrong again. The Allies wrote the treaty and told the Germans to sign or face invasion.

When they saw the treaty, Germans were horrified. Some even wanted to fight on and be crushed rather than accept the humiliating terms in the treaty. They called it the *Diktat* – the dictated peace. The government knew that they could not fight on. To do so would cause great suffering to the German people. On 28 June 1919 the treaty was signed in the Hall of Mirrors in the Palace of Versailles near Paris. A British official described the occasion.

A Through the doors at the end . . . come four officers of France, Great Britain, America and Italy. And then, isolated and pitiable, come the two Germans, Dr Müller, Dr. Bell. The silence is terrifying . . . They keep their eyes fixed away from those two thousand staring eyes, fixed upon the ceiling. They are deathly pale . . . There is general tension. They sign. There is general relaxation . . . We kept our seats while the Germans were conducted like prisoners from the dock.

Harold Nicolson, Peacemaking, 1919.

B The Germans sign the treaty. Note how grand the hall is.

What the Treaty Said

The treaty they signed punished the Germans in several ways.

- Germany lost land to Belgium and to the new country of Poland. She also had to return Alsace and Lorraine to France.

- All of Germany's overseas colonies were taken away.

The treaty also tried to make sure that Germany would never again have the military strength to fight another war.

- The German army was to be limited to only 100,000 men.
- Germany was to have no air force or submarines.
- No German soldiers or weapons were allowed to be placed near the border with France.

These were bad enough, but other points seemed to be meant as insults.

- By the 'War Guilt' clause, Germany had to accept the blame for starting the war.
- Because of this, Germany had to pay reparations. This meant they were to pay to repair the damage done to French and Belgian property during the war.
- All the coal mined in the Saar was to go to France for fifteen years.

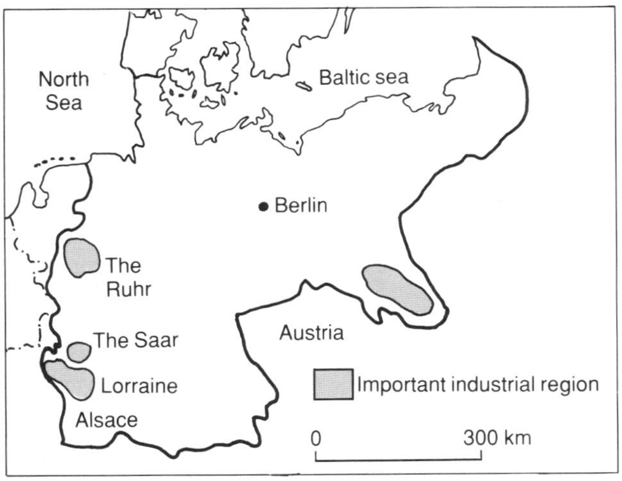

C Germany in 1914.

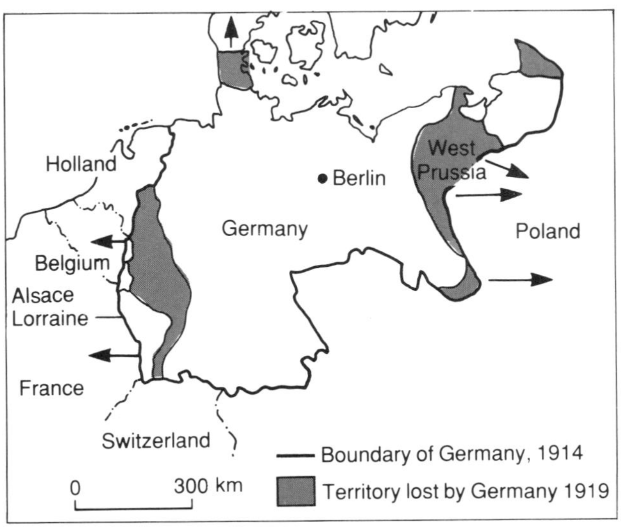

D Germany in 1919.

?

1 Explain in your own words why the Germans expected to take part in drawing up the treaty.

2 Look at sources A and B.
a) In what ways did the Allies humiliate the Germans who were sent to sign the treaty?
b) What is written in source A to suggest that many people in the Hall were not sure that the Germans would sign?

3 Which points in the treaty were meant to:
make it hard for Germany to fight another war?
punish Germany?
make it seem right that Germany *should* be punished?

Group discussion

A treaty can be thought of as a good one if it helps to keep peace in the future. Draw up lists of what your group think were good points about the settlement and bad points about the settlement for keeping the peace.
Does your group think the treaty was a fair one, or not? Give as many reasons as you can for your decision.

ARGUMENTS OVER THE TREATY

Even while it was being drawn up the treaty was the subject of debate. The three leaders who drew up the treaty had very different outlooks.

President Woodrow Wilson of the U.S.A. would have liked a peace settlement that was not too harsh. He wanted to be known as the man who brought a lasting peace to Europe. In contrast, Georges Clemenceau of France had a simple practical aim. He was determined that Germany would be crushed so completely that France need never again fear invasion. The British Prime Minister, David Lloyd George, was caught between his own wish to be fair and the British people's feelings, summed up in slogans like 'Hang the Kaiser', 'Make Germany pay' and 'Squeeze them until the pips squeak'. As the conference was held in the very emotional atmosphere of Paris, there was no doubt which view would win.

When the treaty was published even some of the Allies were shocked. The American Secretary of State, Robert Lansing, wrote:

E The terms of peace appear immeasurably harsh and humiliating, while many of them seem to me impossible of performance.

Memorandum, Robert Lansing.

President Wilson himself was heard to observe that, if he were a German, he would never sign it. Germany's new leaders, however, felt that they had no choice but to sign.

German Reaction to the Treaty

Not surprisingly, there was angry reaction in Germany. It was not just because they had been forced to accept the treaty and the punishments

F Germany after 1919. The shaded areas show where German speaking people lived outside Germany.

it contained. They were also angry because many Germans would now have to live under foreign rule in Poland and Czechoslovakia, and because German-speaking Austria was not allowed to join with Germany.

The *Deutsche Zeitung* (German News) spoke for many on the day the treaty was signed. A black mourning band surrounded the main article.

G

VENGEANCE! GERMAN NATION!

Today in the Hall of mirrors at Versailles, a disgraceful treaty is being signed. Never forget it! On that spot where, in the glorious year of 1871, the German Empire in all its glory began, today German honour is dragged to the grave. Never forget it! The German people with unceasing labour, will push forward to reconquer that place among nations to which they are entitled. Then there will be vengeance for the shame of 1919.

Deutsche Zeitung, *28 June 1919.*

The Kaiser made a similar forecast about the future.

H After years of the heaviest trial will come the liberation from a yoke imposed unjustly upon a great, strong, honest nation. Then every one of us will be glad and proud that he is a German.

Kaiser Wilhelm II, Memoirs.

The man who would try to carry out the Kaiser's hopes saw how he could use the treaty to gain the support of the German people.

I Each one of the points of that Treaty could be branded in the minds and hearts of the German people until sixty million men and women find their souls aflame with a feeling of rage and shame; and a torrent of fire bursts forth as from a furnace, and a will of steel is forged from it, with the common cry – "we will have arms again!"

Adolf Hitler, Mein Kampf.

Criticism of the treaty led its makers to defend their actions. Georges Clemenceau tried to justify the War Guilt clause. He wrote, 'For the catastrophe of 1914 the Germans are responsible. Only a professional liar would deny this.'

Lloyd George told the British Parliament what he thought the treaty had achieved.

J We have disarmed; we have punished. We have demonstrated, I think, to the world . . . that you cannot trample on national rights and liberties, that you cannot break covenants . . .

This is the task which we set ourselves, and I claim that this Treaty will be a lighthouse in the deep, warning nations and the rulers of nations against the perils against which the German Empire shattered itself.

Lloyd George's speech to the House of Commons, 21 July 1919.

The strength of the German reaction dismayed many British and French people. It seemed that the Germans did not realise the position they were in. In later years a British journalist regretted that the Allies had not actually invaded Germany.

K Alas, alas! The mistake, as personally I have never ceased to think, was not to have crossed the Rhine in full massiveness in 1919; not to have dictated at Berlin a more impressive and competent peace. They would have understood then what indisputable defeat means. They don't now.

J.L. Garvin, editor of the Observer, *writing in 1933.*

On the day of its signing, one Scottish newspaper gave a balanced view of the treaty, identifying both hopes and fears for the future.

L If we can see no good reason why we should unduly rejoice over the humiliation of Germany . . . there is ample room for solid satisfaction because of the signing of the Treaty itself . . . It does not even follow that all will run smoothly with Germany herself, far less that she will remain satisfied with the conditions that are imposed upon her; what it means . . . is that Germany . . . has taken a definite step to good understanding with her sister nations.

Kilmarnock Standard, *28 June 1919.*

Policy of Appeasement

The treaty might have held had the Allies been determined to enforce it. Their own sense of guilt over its harshness made British and French governments unwilling to do so. This policy of 'appeasement' helped to encourage German hopes for the scrapping of the treaty. It also encouraged aggressive attitudes and policies in Germany.

This cartoon gives one view of future dangers from appeasement.

PEACE AND FUTURE CANNON FODDER

The Tiger: "Curious! I seem to hear a child weeping!"

M Peace and Cannon Fodder. A *Punch* cartoon from 1919. Clemenceau was nicknamed 'The Tiger' because of his fierce determination that the treaty would satisfy French demands.

?

1 Why were the Germans bitter about the treatment of areas A,B and C in source F?

2 Compare source G and source H.
   a) Quote a phrase from each which shows that both writers thought the treaty was unfair.
   b) '. . . a similar forecast about the future . . .' What did both writers expect to happen?

3 a) What use did Hitler expect to make of the treaty? (Source I.)
   b) Which points did he think the Germans would demand to be removed? Quote a phrase from the extract to support your answer.

4 What lesson did Lloyd George hope the treaty would teach the world? (Source J.)

5 Which evidence in source L suggests that the writer
   a) was doubtful about Germany's attitude to the treaty?
   b) was hopeful about future relations with Germany?

6 Which sources suggest that the Allies were not all happy with the treaty?

7 Look back at your answers to questions 2 and 3. What do you think caused Mr Garvin to make the comments in source K?

8 What prediction did the cartoonist make in source M? Why might this happen?

Debate

Choose four pupils to represent Germany, Great Britain, France and the U.S.A. Each representative should prepare a short speech to explain his or her country's opinion of the treaty. After each person has spoken other members of the group/class may ask them questions or put points to them. At the end of the debate the group/class should vote on whether or not they think the treaty was a fair one.

4 THE WEIMAR REPUBLIC

A New Constitution

On 19 January 1919, thirty million Germans voted for the members of the National Assembly. They met just over a fortnight later in the small city of Weimar in the middle of Germany. The meeting was held there because there was still a danger of violence in Berlin.

The Assembly's job was to write a new constitution for Germany. This would say how governments would be elected, what their powers would be, and what rights people would have.

B So we shall go to work with our grand aim firmly before us, to safeguard the rights of the German people, to set up a strong democracy in Germany . . . We want to build a Reich of justice and truth, based upon the equality of all human beings.

Opening speech by Ebert to the National Assembly, 6 February 1919.

A Weimar. This quiet city was connected more with poetry than with politics.

First, the Assembly elected Ebert as President of the new German Republic. Then its members took several months to debate the details of the constitution. The final version showed that they had tried very hard to protect people's rights. These were set out as 'fundamental laws'.

C The Fundamental Laws.

Personal freedom is guaranteed. No-one can be arrested unless they have broken the law.

The home of every German is a place of safety for him. The authorities cannot enter it without proper cause.

Every German has the right to express his opinion freely by word, writing, printed matter or picture.

All Germans have the right to hold peaceful meetings.

All Germans have the right to form unions and societies.

Property is guaranteed.

?

1 Copy this paragraph, filling in the blanks:
The N________ A________ was elected in 1919. It met in the city of ____________ . This city was chosen because it was ________ , and less likely to be disturbed by violence than ____________ .
The Assembly had to write a new C________ for Germany.

2 a) Monarchy = rule by a king or queen.
Democracy = rule by a parliament elected by the people.
Dictatorship = rule by one person with complete power.
In source B, did Ebert say that Germany should be ruled by:
a single strong ruler?
a king like Kaiser Wilhelm had been?
an elected parliament?
b) From this list, choose *three* words that show what Ebert thought the new constitution should give Germans:

Power	Justice	Wealth
Land	Rights	Peace
Equality	Work	

3 Copy and complete these sentences, using source C:
The new constitution gave the German people protection and rights. They were protected because ____________ and ____________________ .
They had the right to ____________________ and to ____________________ .

*T*HE BURDEN OF DEFEAT

Those who met at Weimar knew that it would be hard to make the new Republic popular. For one thing, many Germans saw its very existence as evidence of national humiliation. As a modern historian has observed,

D In the eyes of many German patriots, the republic was only there at all because Germany had been defeated and the people who founded it had helped in that defeat. The republic had also signed the peace terms (and would always be blamed for them); it had been born in revolution, and had at once to face the awful practical problems of defeat: the demobilisation of the armies when no jobs were available, the feeding of the cities while the Allied blockade was still kept up.

J.M. Roberts, The Age of Upheaval, *1981.*

The Assembly had to reach decisions on controversial issues: the powers of a new head of state; the method of electing the new Parliament (*Reichstag*); and the balance between the powers of central government and those of the Lands (the states like Prussia and Bavaria that many Germans identified with).

E The German Lands.

These issues caused arguments, as politicians had very different views of what the future Germany should be like.

F The Main Parties 1919; some of these were more interested in fighting Communism than in making the Republic work.

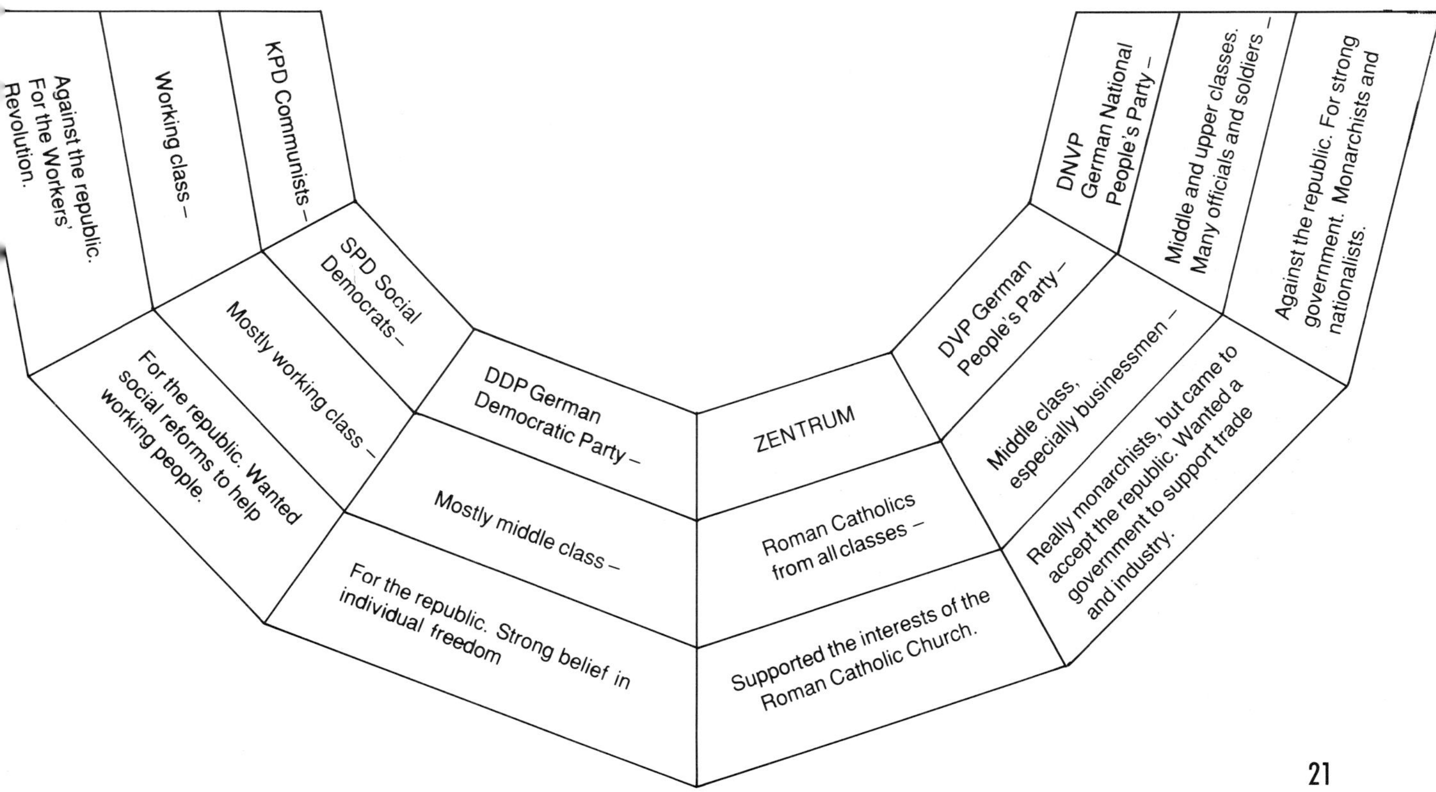

G German People's Party election poster. The caption reads 'Free us from red chains'.

● *The work of the Assembly*

Despite the differences among its members, the Assembly drew up a constitution. Germany became a federal republic under a President. States like Prussia and Bavaria wanted to keep as much power as possible to themselves, because they feared a communist take-over in Berlin. At last, a compromise was reached. The central government had control of taxation and foreign policy, and national laws counted above those of the Lands. The Lands still ran the police, the courts and the schools.

Two criticisms have often been made of the new arrangements for ruling Germany. First, the President was given special powers.

H Where public security and order are . . . endangered . . ., the President . . . may take the measures necessary for their restoration, intervening if necessary with the help of armed forces. For this purpose he is permitted, for the time being, to set aside . . . the fundamental laws . . . Such measures shall be withdrawn upon the demand of the Reichstag.

Article 48 of the Weimar Constitution, 1919.

One man having so much power could be very dangerous.

The second criticism concerned the method of electing the Reichstag. The Reichstag was elected every four years. All men and women over 20 were entitled to vote, by secret ballot. Parties named lists of candidates in each of the 38 districts, and people voted for the party list, not for individual candidates. One name from the list was elected for every sixty thousand votes for the party. This was a fair system, as the parties won seats in the Reichstag in proportion to the votes cast, but no party ever had a majority on its own. This meant that all governments were coalitions, usually involving several parties. Some people have argued that this made the governments weak. The Republic itself seemed weak to Germans who had been used to strong leadership under the Kaiser.

Election by proportional representation also helped extremist parties like the Nazis. Even if they could only attract a fairly small number of voters, they were likely to gain a few seats in the Reichstag. This meant that Nazi ideas would be heard in the national parliament, and this helped them to grow from a local pressure group into a national party.

By assisting such groups (some of which were dedicated to the overthrow of democracy) to be represented in the Reichstag, the new constitution made it more difficult for the Republic to defend itself against its enemies. There were more than enough of these to make democracy very fragile indeed.

I Friedrich Ebert, the SPD leader who became the first President of the Weimar Republic. Many people see him as the founder of democratic government in Germany.

?

1 Using sources D-G, give as many reasons as you can why it was difficult to write a constitution that would attract the loyalty of all Germans.

2 a) In what circumstances was the President granted special powers? (Source H.)

b) Who was to judge whether or not these circumstances had occurred?

c) Compare source H with source C. What were the implications of these powers for ordinary Germans?

d) What safeguard seems to be built in to prevent abuse of these powers? Do you think it was likely to be effective? Explain your answer.

3 Look back at source B. How successful do you think the Assembly was in fulfilling Ebert's aims?

Role play

Study the following character sketches of imaginary Germans. Decide which party you think each would have supported in 1919, and what she/he would have thought of the Republic. In your group/class, cast one person in each role, and act out a scene in which they discuss the new republic.

Liesl Vogts – wife of a civil servant. Her son was killed on the Somme in 1916.

Josef Held – sailor who took part in the mutiny in November 1918. He is angry about the murders of Liebknecht and Luxemburg.

Gerda Pfeffer – widow of a carpenter, she is a regular at Mass in the village Roman Catholic Church.

Magda Wentz – a part-time factory worker, who lives in a tenement flat with her parents. Her father is unemployed.

Kurt Adler – a Jewish shopkeeper, who hopes for a fair society in the new Germany.

5 THE NAZIS

● *The Leader*

The man who took advantage of the weaknesses of the Republic was not even born in Germany. Adolf Hitler was the son of a civil servant from the small town of Braunau, in Austria.

At school, Hitler's record was poor. On leaving, he went to Vienna, hoping to get into the Academy of Fine Arts, but he failed the entrance examination. He scraped a living by taking casual jobs, like colouring picture postcards. In Vienna, he came across many racist ideas, including hatred of the Jews, which became important in Nazi beliefs.

By the time war broke out in 1914, Hitler was living in Munich, in southern Germany. He volunteered at once, and fought in France and Belgium. In his dangerous job as a runner, carrying messages between his Company and Headquarters, he was wounded and later gassed. He won the Iron Cross twice and was promoted to corporal.

When the war ended Hitler was in hospital, recovering from the effects of gas on his eyes. He was horrified at Germany's defeat. He blamed the Jews and politicians, saying that they had betrayed the soldiers.

● *A New Party*

Back in Munich, Hitler took a job as an army spy. He was sent to report on a group called the German Workers' Party. Soon he saw that he might be able to use this party to push his own ideas, so he joined.

A Hitler as a young politician. Notice the neat suit, collar and tie, slicked back hair, and his expression.

Almost at once he found he had a talent for public speaking.

B When the man stepped forward on the platform, there was almost no applause . . . Then he began to speak, quietly . . . at first. Before long his voice had risen to a hoarse shriek that gave an extraordinary effect . . . Leaning [forward] . . . he was holding the masses, and me with them, under a hypnotic spell by the sheer force of his conviction . . . I do not know how to describe the emotions that swept over me as I heard this man . . . When he spoke of the disgrace of Germany, I felt ready to spring on any enemy.

Kurt Ludecke, I Knew Hitler, *1938.*

C Hitler practising a speech in front of a mirror.

He rose quickly to lead the group. On 5 February 1920 he changed its name to the National Socialist German Workers' Party. The Nazi party had been born.

?

1 a) Source A was taken as a publicity photograph. Pick out *three* things that suggest Hitler wanted to appear respectable.
b) Look at his expression. Choose the word from this list that you think describes it best:
excited determined
friendly sad angry
c) Why do you think he put on that expression for the camera?

2 What evidence is there in source B that Hitler was a powerful speaker?

3 In source C, Hitler is shown in a dramatic pose. Why do you think he used his hands and arms like this in his speeches?

*T*HE PARTY PROGRAMME

From the start, the new party made its policies very clear. Its programme was built around nationalism, racist theories and a belief in strong government.

D

1. We demand the union of all Germans in one Great Germany by the right of self-determination of peoples.
3. We demand land and territory (colonies) for the feeding of our people and for the settlement of our surplus population.
4. Only those who are members of the nation can be citizens. Only those who are of German blood . . . can be members of the nation. No Jew can, therefore, be a member of the nation.
20. . . . An understanding of national

consciousness must be taught to the children at the earliest possible age.

25. For the carrying out of all these we demand: the creation of a strong central power in the Reich.

Programme of the Nazi party, 1920.

This programme proved that the Nazis were enemies of democratic government. They were not only opponents of the existing parties; they meant to topple the Weimar Republic itself. Hitler had already made his views on democracy plain. It was weak. It was Jewish. It was *not* German.

The National Socialists were not the only right-wing group to feel this way. Only a month after their formation there was an attempt to seize power in Berlin, led by a civilian called Wolfgang Kapp and supported by some nationalists, rebellious sailors and *Freikorps* members. The government had to leave Berlin, and the revolt was only defeated when the trade unions called a general strike in the city. Then in 1922 nationalists assassinated the Foreign Minister, Walter Rathenau, who was Jewish. There was a lot of potential support for Hitler.

THE BROWNSHIRTS

Like most parties in Germany in the 1920s, the Nazis formed their own private army. At first its nature was disguised, but its purpose was not.

E The NSDAP has created its own gymnastic and sports section . . . It is intended to bind our young party members together . . . It is intended to provide protection for the propaganda activity of the leaders. But above all it is intended to develop in the hearts of our young supporters a tremendous desire for action, to drive home to them and burn into them the fact that history does not make men, but men history.

Nazi party newspaper, 3 August 1921.

F S.A. members in 1923.

G Nazi propaganda poster of 1941. The image had not changed since the 1920s. The German caption said 'Service in the S.A. develops comradeship, toughness, strength.'

This new force was soon named the *Sturm Abteilung*, the Storm Section (S.A.). It was given a uniform with a military-style brown shirt, and trained in army fashion. Its first jobs were to protect Nazi speakers, to prevent opponents from breaking up Nazi meetings, and to disrupt meetings held by other parties. Anxious to project an image of youth and vigour, it was not long before the S.A. became involved in violence as they tried to drive their enemies, especially the Communists, from the streets.

As early as October 1922 Hitler led 700 S.A. men, complete with banners and a band, to a 'German Day' parade in the town of Coburg, where they were intercepted by Communists.

H We met a great storm of insults from a crowd collected by the Reds to hoot at us . . .

The S.A. men kept strict formation and ignored the jeers . . . The turmoil and tension reached a climax when the crowds, incited by agitators, began to throw things and to attack us bodily. Patience could endure no more; now we had to defend ourselves . . .

For nearly a quarter of an hour it was an outright battle, man to man. At first the police took no sides, striking at everyone with impartial vigour. But soon, probably because they shared our enthusiastic dislike for the street rabble, most of them took our side, and before long we were master of the field.

Kurt Ludecke, I Knew Hitler.

This was one of the first of many such clashes in which young Nazis had the chance to prove themselves.

In its early days, the NSDAP was hardly known outside the state of Bavaria. There, in 1923, Hitler saw his first chance to take advantage of the terrible problems ordinary people were facing as the German economy began to collapse.

?

1. Which of Hitler's youthful experiences are likely to have influenced the ideas in the Nazi party programme? Explain your answer.
2. Which parts of the programme (source D) show that the Nazis were (i) racist (ii) authoritarian (iii) nationalist?
3. Look back at source E in chapter 4, p.21. Which other parties would you expect to be (i) allies (ii) enemies of the Nazis? Explain your choice.
4. For what reasons was 1920 a promising time to form a party like the NSDAP?
5. What evidence is there in sources E, F, G and H that the S.A. was intended to be an aggressive organisation?

6 PROBLEMS IN GERMANY

Inflation

War and blockade had hurt the German economy. The loss of colonies and industrial land demanded by the Versailles treaty had made things worse. Now Germany had to pay France and Belgium £100 million a year for 66 years to repair war damage. Most of this had to be paid in goods – coal, iron and timber.

People began to suffer as goods ran short. Prices rose. The government tried to pay its debts by printing more money. This just made prices rise faster, until they were out of control. This is called inflation.

A

Number of Marks to the Dollar	(rounded off)
July 1914	4
July 1920	40
July 1921	80
July 1922	500
January 1923	18,000
July 1923	350,000
September 1923	100,000,000
November 1923	4.000,000,000,000

The face value of banknotes changed nearly every day – hundreds of marks, thousands, millions. By the middle of 1923 they were really worth nothing. People got rid of them for goods, *any* goods. They could always be exchanged for something else later.

B Postage Stamps 1921 – 1923.

2 marks

50 marks

200 marks

75,000 marks

1 million marks

100 million marks

These stamps were overprinted to save printing new ones.

2 million marks on 200 mark stamp.

10,000 million marks on 50 million mark stamp.

C Two women were going to the bank with a washing basket, filled with notes. They passed a shop and saw a crowd standing around the window, put down the basket for a moment and hurried forward to see if there was anything that could be bought. Then they turned round and found that all the notes were there, untouched. But the basket had gone.

A woman remembers life in Berlin, 1923.

Results

Inflation had a dreadful effect on the standard of living of ordinary Germans. Factories closed and unemployment grew. As the prices of food, clothing and fuel rose people went cold and hungry. Disease began to spread.

Those who suffered worst were the middle classes. The workers had little to lose. Many of the middle classes had been fairly well off. Now they were as poor as the workers. They were ashamed and angry. Of course, they blamed the government.

?

1. Copy and complete this paragraph.
   Three reasons why the German economy was in trouble after the war were:
   (i) ______________________ .
   (ii) ______________________ .
   (iii) ______________________ .
2. What does source C tell you about life in Germany in 1923?
3. In what way do sources C and D agree about how inflation affected life in Germany?
4. Using sources A,B and D explain why people no longer wanted money in 1923.

Group discussion

Look back at the characters in the role play in chapter 4, p.23. Which of these people do you think would have been hurt most by the inflation? Explain why you think so.

D Wages being taken in washing baskets to workers.

INFLATION AND DISCONTENT

By 1921 there was ample cause for discontent in Germany. The final reparations figure stunned everyone. They demanded to know how German agriculture and industry were supposed to produce enough to meet the needs of their own people and the requirements of the Allies as well. Their anger was turned on the politicians of the Weimar Republic. In the 1920 elections moderate parties lost support to the Nationalists and the Independent Socialists. Political violence continued, with assassinations commonplace.

THE RÜHR OCCUPATION

Early in 1923 German anger was turned outwards. France had complained that Germany had not kept up deliveries of goods due as reparations payments. In February, French and Belgian troops occupied the industrial area of the Rühr to enforce deliveries.

The German government at once ordered a policy of passive resistance. It told workers, businessmen and officials to refuse to co-operate.

The French reacted by trying to cut off the Rühr from the rest of Germany. They arrested many people, and expelled civil servants, police and others. By humiliating people they caused great bitterness.

E 'No! I will not be forced.' A German miner refuses to work, though threatened by French soldiers.

F We received appropriate rules of conduct at school; but we all knew that none of us would ever salute a French officer. Better hide behind a strange doorway than doff our caps to the enemy.

Theodore Abel, then a schoolboy in Wiesbaden.

These policies brought the German people together, supporting the government against the common foe. Their resolution was strengthened when frustration among the occupying troops led to violent clashes resulting in several deaths. Germans also resented the presence of black soldiers from French African colonies among the forces of occupation. For the moment, national divisions were disguised by hatred of the common enemy.

INFLATION OUT OF CONTROL

Passive resistance had disastrous economic effects. The government tried to pay the strikers and those who had suffered financially, like the mine owners. This forced it to print more and more paper money, whose value collapsed.

In these circumstances, living conditions suffered. Meat consumption per person was half its pre-war level; coal, clothing and soap were almost unobtainable; overcrowding in slum areas made basic hygiene impossible. The Department of Health reported increases in food poisoning as people were reduced to eating rotting food, and malnutrition was widespread.

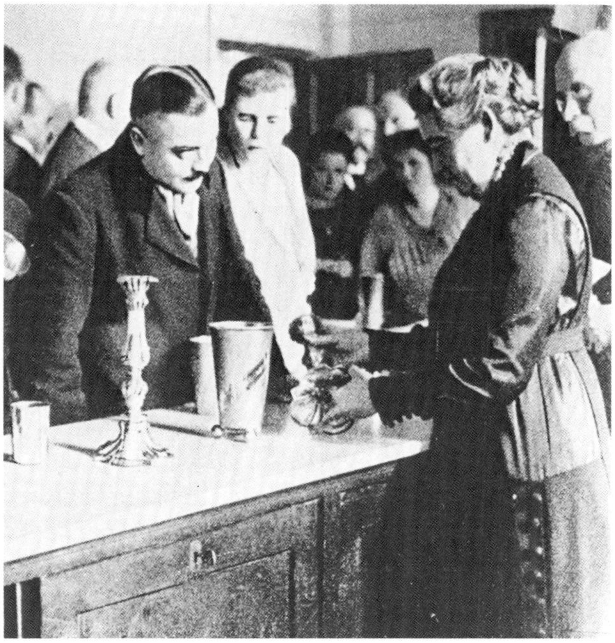

G Brought down by inflation, middle-class citizens survive by selling their valuables.

It was hard for ordinary people to understand what was happening to them. One person, lucky to find a job at all, might work all hours for a wage that could not feed and clothe his family. Another, whose savings had seemed security for old age, might find them worth next to nothing. Herr Neisse worked as a gardener in Berlin, saving to get married.

H There was no doubt in his mind that the disaster which befell him . . . in 1923 was the result of some dire and treasonable plot. His savings, Hilde's savings, their plot of land, their humble enough hopes, had vanished into thin air overnight . . . "With my savings I was able to buy just one cup and saucer which I gave to Hilde instead of her marriage lines . . ." The loss of his bank account had not only shattered whatever faith he might have had in constitutional government, but also struck at the root of his very being, his self-respect, and his right to be respected.

Christabel Bielenberg, The Past is Myself, *1984.*

He was not the only one to lose faith in constitutional government. As one historian has observed:

I Widows, civil servants, teachers, army officers and pensioners lost their lifetime savings . . . It was the scar that never healed. These were the people who later turned to Adolf Hitler.

Louis L. Snyder, The Weimar Republic, *1966.*

Many of these were also the people whose support was critical for the survival of democracy. Their loss of faith threatened to undermine the Republic, as the 1924 election results showed. As for Herr Neisse, in 1931 he joined the Nazi party.

J Reichstag Election Results.

	1920	1924	
German Democratic Party	44	28	moderate parties
German People's Party	62	44	
Social Democrats	113	100	
Communists	2	62	extremist parties
Nazis	0	32	

?

Group discussion

1 Consider these issues as a group. Report back to the class on your conclusions.
   a) Give as many reasons as you can why the German people were discontented by 1923. Classify these under the headings:
   Political Economic Social
   b) Which groups in Germany were worst affected by the inflation? Why was *their* discontent so dangerous for democracy in Germany?

2 As a group, make a wallchart to illustrate the crisis of 1923. You might include a graph of the value of the mark, cartoons or pictures, or a poster bringing out the effects of the crisis on ordinary people.

3 Which of the sources have you found most helpful in understanding the effects of the inflation, and why?

7 THE MUNICH PUTSCH

Hitler's Chance

The people of Bavaria in southern Germany were mostly Roman Catholics. Many were more loyal to Bavaria than to Germany. When the inflation came, some of the leaders planned to rise against the government in Berlin.

A The state of Bavaria.

The Putsch

On 8 November 1923, Herr von Kahr, head of the Bavarian government, spoke at a big meeting in a beer cellar in Munich. General von Lossow (the army Commander in Bavaria) and Colonel von Seisser (the police chief) were with him. Hitler decided to use their meeting to try to seize power.

With some friends, Hitler went into the meeting. He waited until 600 S.A. men had surrounded the building. When Hermann Göring and 25 of them burst into the hall, Hitler jumped onto a chair and fired a shot into the air. He said that a national revolution had begun.

Hitler forced the three leaders into a side room at gunpoint. They refused to join him, but Hitler went back into the hall and announced that they *had* done. His bluff worked. The crowd cheered him. After General Ludendorff arrived to support Hitler, Kahr, Lossow and Seisser agreed to work with him. Hitler spoke to the crowd.

B The government of the November Criminals . . . are declared to be removed. A new national government will be named this very day in Munich . . . The task of the . . . National Government is to organise the march on . . . Berlin, and save the German people.

Speech by Hitler, 8 November 1923.

Then Hitler made a mistake. He left the beer cellar to sort out a fight between some S.A. men and ordinary soldiers. At once Lossow and Kahr ordered the army to put down the Nazi rising.

Defeat

While Hitler was at the beer cellar, Nazis took over government buildings.

C S.A. men prepare to advance.

At the war ministry the army trapped a group headed by the S.A. leader, Ernst Röhm. On the morning of 9 November, Hitler and Ludendorff led a march to the rescue.

As they marched down a narrow street, they were met by the police. Someone fired, and fighting began. It lasted only a minute, but sixteen Nazis and three policemen were killed. Hitler was dragged to the ground with a dislocated shoulder. Some friends drove him off in a car, but two days later he was arrested. Hitler and Ludendorff went on trial for treason.

?

1 In what ways was Bavaria different from the rest of Germany?

2 Explain why Hitler's attempt to seize power
(i) went well at first
(ii) failed in the end.

3 What evidence in source B suggests that the Nazis meant to take over the whole of Germany, and not just Bavaria?

Imaginative writing

4 Using information from the text and sources to help you, write a newspaper report describing the rebellion. You should mention
– what the Nazis did
– how well they were prepared
– how the rebellion was put down.
Give your report a headline.

*H*ITLER ON TRIAL

Hitler's trial provided a portrait in miniature of the obstacles to the growth of democracy in Germany. It demonstrated clearly the nationalist, conservative bias of the forces of law and order.

Past rebellions by left-wing groups like the Spartacists had been put down ruthlessly. Now the leader of an attempted revolution was allowed by the judges to turn his trial into a publicity stunt. In front of a large number of foreign journalists, Hitler interrupted and insulted the witnesses, and made long speeches in which he attacked the Weimar Republic and declared his intention of being a dictator. He made prophecies:

D I believe that the hour will come when the people, who today stand in the street with our swastika banner, will join with those who fired upon them. I believe that this blood will not always separate us. When I learned that it was the police who fired, I was happy that it was not the army . . . One day the hour will come when the army will stand at our side, officers and men.

Hitler speaking at his trial.

He dared the judges to punish him:

E It is not you, gentlemen, who pass judgement on us. That judgement is spoken by the eternal court of history . . . That court will judge us . . . as Germans who wanted only the good of their own people and Fatherland; who wanted to fight and die. You may say we are guilty a thousand times over, but the goddess of the eternal court of history will smile and tear to tatters . . . the sentence of this court. For she acquits us.

Hitler's closing speech.

It was impossible for the court to find Hitler innocent, for he had gloried in his guilt. He was given the minimum possible sentence, five years' imprisonment, which meant that he might be out on parole after six months. Ludendorff, the old war hero, was released at once.

F Ludendorff and Hitler pose together at the end of the trial.

*H*ITLER IN PRISON

Hitler's jail was the fortress of Landsberg, fifty miles west of Munich. His surroundings were pleasant, and he and the other Nazis imprisoned with him suffered few restrictions.

G Hitler and his companions in their common room.

H Hitler's cell in Landsberg fortress.

I Lunch with his fellow-prisoners . . . with Hitler presiding sounded more like a social affair. In the afternoon one prisoner served tea to the others in their cells. Before and after the six o'clock supper . . . they were again free to exercise in the garden for an hour or so.

Kurt Ludecke describes the routine at Landsberg.

During the eight months which he actually served in prison, Hitler spent most of his time writing. The result was his book *Mein Kampf* (*My Struggle*) in which he described his early years and explained his political ideas. He made plain his belief in a revived Germany under a strong leader (himself, of course), his racist ideas of creating a pure 'Aryan' master race by disposing of 'unclean' elements (especially the Jews), and his conviction that Germany must obtain Lebensraum, (Living space), for its people by conquest in eastern Europe.

Most people ignored *Mein Kampf*. Its heavy style made it difficult to read, and those who persevered thought it was too wild to be taken seriously as a political statement. They were wrong, as Hitler would prove when he became dictator.

?

1 Why were Hitler's trial and sentence evidence of democracy's weakness in Germany?

2 In source D (i) what evidence is there that Hitler believed the police would eventually come to support the Nazis?
(ii) what evidence is there of Hitler's affection for the army?

3 What do you think Hitler's purpose was in addressing the judges in the tone of source E? Explain your answer.

4 What evidence do sources E and F provide that Hitler was proud of his actions?

5 Comment on Hitler's treatment in prison, as revealed by sources G,H and I.

Imaginative writing

6 Write an account of Hitler's trial, as though you were one of the foreign journalists who were present. Your report should describe what happened, and comment on the implications of the trial for the future of German democracy.

8 YEARS OF HOPE 1924-1929

Recovery

Inflation could not be allowed to go on for ever. The outside world could not risk the consequences of complete collapse in Germany. An American banker, Charles Dawes, was given the job of preparing a plan to help Germany recover.

With the agreement of the Allies, Dawes arranged for the annual reparations bill to be reduced, and for huge American loans to help German industry and trade to regain their strength. The old currency was replaced by a new mark, whose value was guaranteed. The coal and steel industries were modernised. This plan was so successful that, by 1927, Germany was producing more goods than in 1913, despite the losses of Versailles. The country began to show at least a few signs of prosperity. This prosperity began to be visible in everyday life.

A A wonderful ferment was working in Germany. Life seemed more free, more modern, more exciting than any place I had ever seen . . . And everywhere the accent was on youth . . . They were a healthy, carefree, sun-worshipping lot and they were filled with an enormous zest for living to the full and in complete freedom.

A young American journalist recalls life in Germany in 1925.

International Relations

In other ways, too, Germans were regaining their self respect. Under the guidance of the foreign minister, Gustav Stresemann, Germany began to achieve recognition from other powers. In 1925 the Locarno Treaty guaranteed the borders with France and Belgium, and in the following year Germany was invited to join the League of Nations. The Allies also agreed to reduce the forces occupying the Rhineland. Stresemann's personal part in improving international relations was recognised in 1926 when he was awarded the Nobel Peace Prize.

Results

These advances began to create hope that the Weimar Republic might succeed after all. This was reinforced by the results of the 1928 election, in which the Social Democrats, who were most strongly committed to the Republic, did much better than they had done in either of the two elections in 1924. The nationalist parties lost ground, but so did the middle-class parties whose supporters had suffered so much in the inflation. Though the Nazis did badly, a warning that extremists were still dangerous could be seen in the success of the Communists.

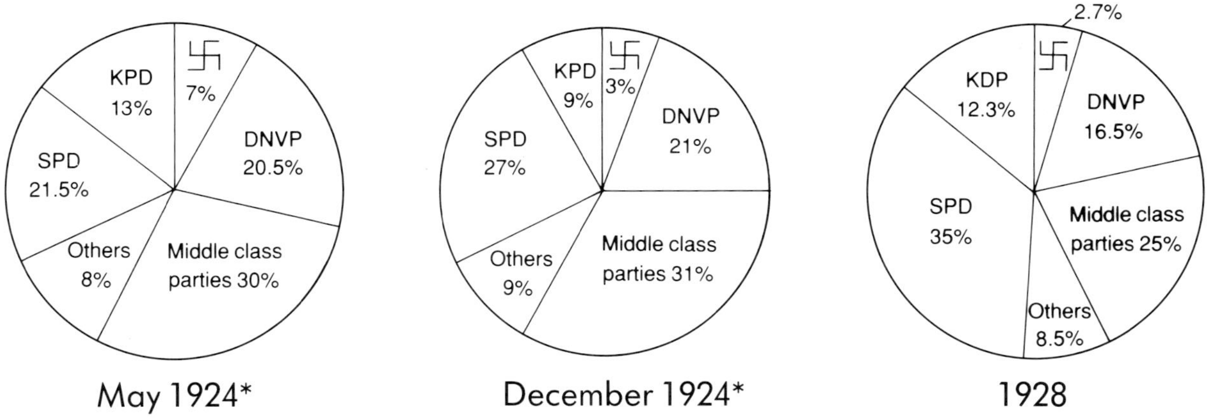

B Proportions of Seats in the Reichstag.
* During the elections of 1924 the Nazi party was illegal, so its candidates called themselves 'Racialists'.

Though democratic government was less unpopular by 1928, its hold on the German people was very fragile. It depended utterly on the economic revival continuing. But the revival itself was very precarious. It in turn depended too heavily on foreign help, and especially on American loans. If anything were to compel the withdrawal of these loans, the results would be disastrous for Germany in every sense. Since his release from prison in December 1924, Adolf Hitler had been preparing carefully to take advantage of any such disaster.

?

1 Why was Germany able to recover from the crisis of 1923?

2 What evidence was there that life in Germany was improving in the second half of the 1920s? (Use information from the text and source A).

3 What signs of hope could be found by comparing the election results of 1924 and 1928? (Source B.) What warning did the results contain?

4 Why do you think the Nazis were not as successful in 1928 as they had been in 1924?

C The Locarno honeymoon. This photograph shows European leaders and their wives after the signing of the Locarno Treaty in 1925.

9 VOTE FOR HITLER!

The Lessons of Failure

Hitler had tried to seize power once by using violence. He had failed. He decided to give up the idea of revolution. Instead, he would persuade people to vote him into power.

A Instead of working to gain power by arms, we shall have to hold our noses and enter the Reichstag against the Catholic and Marxist members. If outvoting them takes longer than outshooting them, at least the results will be guaranteed . . . Sooner or later we shall have a majority, and after that we shall have Germany.

Hitler speaking to a friend in Landsberg prison.

B Hitler in S.A. uniform with standard bearer.

To get the votes, the party had to be organised. There were to be local branches in as many towns and villages as possible. In this way everyone would hear what the Nazis had to say, and have the chance to vote for them if they wanted.

Winning Support

The first thing that Hitler wanted was to give people a good image of the Nazis.

He dressed the S.A. in smart uniforms. He had them drilled to march well behind the swastika flag. He wanted them to look young, neat and strong. This would attract people to listen to what they had to say. What the Nazis had to say would be simple.

C The masses* can learn little and understand little. All propaganda must be limited to a few slogans. These slogans should be repeated until the very last person has got hold of the message.

Adolf Hitler, Mein Kampf.

*masses = ordinary people

Here are the main points of the message.

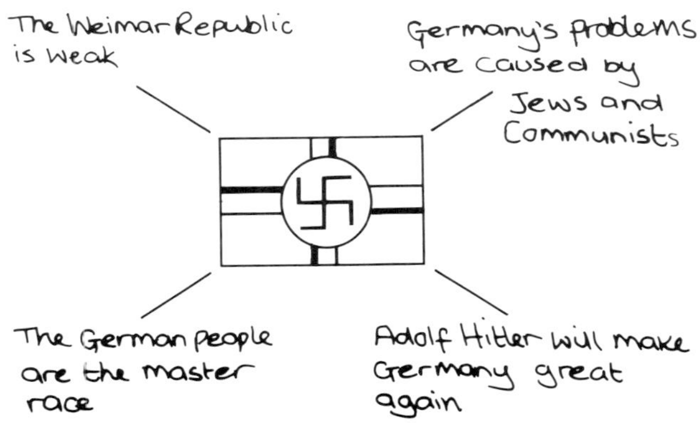

Nazi speakers screamed the message at big public meetings. Nazi newspapers carried it in large print. Nazi posters advertised it everywhere. More and more people began to believe it.

D Nazi open air meeting. Note the lorry loads of stormtroopers.

?

1 Copy and complete this passage.
Hitler's failure at Munich taught him that he would not win power by using ________ . Instead, he would try to have Nazis elected to the R________ . He would take power by ______ his enemies.

2 In source A (i) what words show that Hitler did not like the idea of going into the Reichstag? (ii) what evidence is there that he knew he would not win quickly?

3 In what ways does source B support the idea that Hitler wanted the Nazis to have a good image?

4 Why did Hitler want the Nazi message to be spread using slogans? (Source C.)

5 a) What methods did the Nazis use to put across their ideas?
b) Why do you think there were stormtroopers at the election meeting shown in source D?

*R*EORGANISING THE PARTY

At first, the activities of the National Socialist party had been mostly in Bavaria. To be a party of the whole nation, its members had to be known throughout Germany. This required a national organisation, which was built up between 1924 and 1929.

Hitler divided Germany up into regions based on Reichstag electoral districts. Each was called a Gau, and had its own party leader, or Gauleiter.

Party Headquarters

↑

Gau – (Regional Headquarters) One in each electoral district

↑

Kreis – District Organisation

↑

Local Branches – from 15 members to several hundred

E Nazi Organisation 1929.

The local branches held meetings and handed out leaflets. Although progress might be slow, this provided a good framework for action when the opportunity came.

At the same time, Hitler settled a number of quarrels which had threatened to split the party while he was in prison. Quickly he achieved total control over the party, which accepted the Führerprinzip (leadership principle) as a key part of its policy.

*P*ROPAGANDA

With the help of Dr Josef Goebbels, a publicity expert, Hitler now tried to sell his party to the German people, just as advertisers sell goods. Hitler's instinct told him which approach to favour.

F He knew that a politically uneducated mass public was bound to be receptive to emotive appeal rather than to rational argument. Propaganda had to concentrate on as few points as possible, it had to hammer them home repeatedly, it had to present them in terms of black and white. It could make no concessions to the other side.

Z.A.B. Zeman, Nazi Propaganda, *1973.*

He also knew that the most powerful method of influencing people was by speaking to them directly. This was convenient, for his greatest talent was oratory.

G His rasping voice rarely failed to exert an uncanny hypnotic effect on the audience . . . He never reasoned with audiences but simply put into words what they were longing to hear, feeding on their hidden anxieties . . . and forcing his listeners to surrender their will to that of the leader.

William Carr, A History of Germany 1815-1945, *1979.*

Hitler took advantage of this gift by addressing as many public meetings as possible. The party also trained speakers to travel the country and spread the Nazi message. Their talks concentrated on local issues. Often the politics followed an event of some sort.

H Frequently such propaganda squads stay in a certain place for several days and try to win the population for the movement through the most varied sorts of entertainment such as concerts, sports days . . . and even church parades.

Report, Prussian Ministry of the Interior, May 1930.

Other parades were central to the Nazi campaign. The smart uniforms of the S.A. were highly visible on the streets.

I S.A. parade in Munich.

J Nazi poster, 'National Race for S.A.' On the left, young people salute the troops; in the middle, a priest raises his hands in prayer; on the right a capitalist grasps at the S.A. man's leg.

The Brownshirts had several functions. They helped to provide the party with a youthful, virile, disciplined image in the military tradition, so familiar to Germans.

L The S.A. will appear in public only in closed formation . . . The sight of a large number of men inwardly and outwardly uniform and disciplined, whose total commitment to fighting is clear or can be sensed, makes the deepest impression on every German.

S.A. Order number 3, November 1926.

They were also used to spice the propaganda campaign with a dash of intimidation. They broke up opponents' meetings and protected their own, and picked street fights at favourable odds with enemy private armies, especially the Communist Red Front. By giving people nightmares on the one hand, and promising them their dreams on the other, the Nazis hoped to build support.

● *Methods of Publicity*

Apart from the spoken word, the Nazis used a variety of methods to gain publicity. Even the marches and rallies had a visual side, with Nazi symbols shown off proudly.

K A Nazi rally.

Visual propaganda was not limited to the display of symbols. Nazi slogans appeared on walls, and the party made widespread use of posters to put across their ideas.

During that campaign Goebbels ordered triple the usual number of copies of party newspapers to be printed, with two-thirds of them being distributed free.

M Propaganda posters from the 1932 election campaign. The posters on the left promise freedom for children and those on the right promise work and bread.

The Nazis exploited the mass media. The *Völkischer Beobachter* bought in Munich in 1920 was only the first of many Nazi newspapers published throughout Germany. In 1929 Hitler was fortunate enough to impress the Nationalist leader, Alfred Hugenberg, who owned a chain of cinemas. The two men agreed to co-operate in a campaign against a new plan to amend reparations payments, the Young Plan. Although the campaign failed, Nazi meetings were featured in newsreels in Hugenberg's cinemas across Germany. It was wonderful publicity.

Even more spectacular was the 'Hitler over Germany' campaign during the 1932 Presidential election, when Hitler visited 21 towns in six days.

N A critical innovation: the Leader will conduct this next campaign by 'plane. By this means he will be able to speak three or four times a day at various places . . . and address about one and a half million people in spite of the time being so short.

Dr Josef Goebbels' diary, 18 March 1932.

TARGETS

In its early years the movement tried to win working-class support in the cities. Progress was slow, for most remained loyal to the working-class parties – the Social Democrats and Communists.

From about 1927, the Nazis took their attention away from the cities. They noticed that farmers were suffering from low prices for their produce, so they developed new policies aimed at the countryside and small towns. They blamed the banks and, of course, the Jews for the farmers' troubles, and promised them lower taxes and rents. They also found out that meetings were more successful in smaller centres.

O In small towns and villages mass meetings with good speakers are events and are often talked about for weeks, while in big cities the effect of meetings with even three or four thousand people soon disappear.

Völkischer Beobachter, 31 May 1928.

By 1930 13.2 per cent of party members were farmers.

The Nazis also turned their propaganda on the middle classes. They had special leaflets highlighting the problems of small businessmen, craftsmen and shopkeepers. They told these people they were being exploited for the benefit of the Weimar politicians. They told them their businesses were being ruined by Jewish big business.

P Nazi cartoon, entitled 'The Jewish department store eats up German shopkeepers'.

Here, too, the Nazis were successful, for in the elections in 1930 and 1932 it was the middle-class parties which lost most support to the Nazis.

Source interpretation

In these activities you will be asked to practise some of the skills historians use in dealing with sources. These include

- extracting relevant information to answer questions
- comparing sources to evaluate a historical interpretation
- assessing the value of sources
- assessing whether or not a source is biased.

1. Compare sources, D,E,H and O. Explain fully how the NSDAP used its organisation to publicise its views as widely as possible throughout Germany.
2. In what way do sources C and F agree about Hitler's approach to propaganda?
3. How does source G suggest he put this approach into practice? Look at sources B and C in chapter 5, pages 24–25. What evidence in source B supports Carr's interpretation? Which techniques illustrated in these sources helped Hitler to achieve the effects described by Carr?
4. What part did the S.A. play in Nazi propaganda? (Sources D,I,J,L.)
5. By what means did the Nazis attempt to reach as many people as possible with their message? Why were they most successful in smaller communities? (Sources K,M,N,O.)
6. Compare sources J and P. What evidence is there that both artists were biased in favour of the Nazis?
7. Why is source M a useful one for historians? To answer a question like this about a picture it is helpful to consider (i) what the picture shows. Does it contain significant information about the subject?
(ii) whether there is evidence of bias. Has the picture been posed specially, perhaps to make someone look impressive, or has the photographer or artist tried to catch the person in an undignified position?
(iii) whether there is internal evidence to allow you to date the event shown.
8. Now choose one of the events described in chapter 7 or chapter 8. Design *two* posters, one showing the event from a Nazi point of view and one as though drawn by an enemy of the NSDAP.

10 THE NAZIS COME TO POWER

● *Depression*

In October 1929 the value of shares on the American Stock Exchange suddenly collapsed. Many of the people who owned them lost fortunes. This was also true of banks, which had millions of dollars in shares.

These banks had lent money to factory owners, shopkeepers, traders and other business people. Now they asked them to repay the money. Many could not, and had to close down.

The Americans had lent money to other countries as well, including Germany. These countries, too, had to pay back their loans. As a result, there was less trade, factories closed, and unemployment grew. In this depression, Germany suffered dreadfully.

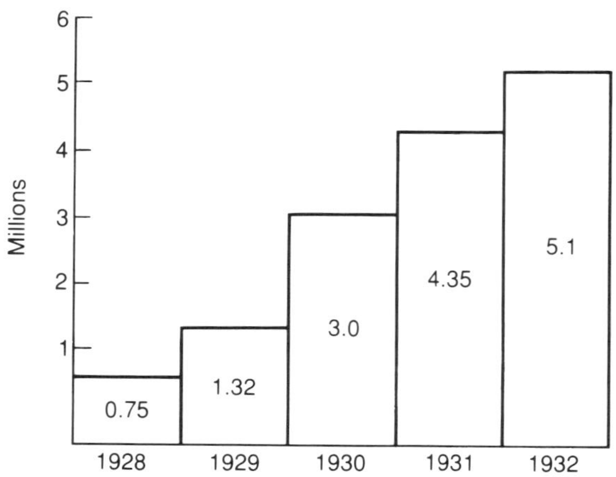

A Unemployment in Germany.

B Translate these figures into terms of men standing helplessly on the street corners of every industrial town in Germany; of houses without food and warmth; of boys and girls leaving school without any chance of a job, and one may begin to guess something of the . . . anxiety and embitterment burned into the minds of ordinary German working men and women.

Alan Bullock, Hitler: A Study in Tyranny, *1962.*

The coalition governments of the Republic seemed unable to solve the problem. The parties which formed them began to fall out. First one government resigned, then another. People started to lose what faith they had left in the system. More and more people were willing to listen to those who claimed to have a simple solution for Germany's troubles. Some turned to the Communists; others were happy to hear Hitler's promises.

C Nazi poster. The German words say 'Our last hope. Hitler.'

● *Mistakes*

Nazi support showed in elections. In 1928 less than a million people voted for them, but in 1930 they got nearly 6.5 million votes and in July 1932 over 13.5 million. By then, they were the largest party in the Reichstag, though they could not form a government alone.

Others saw how popular they were, and hoped to use them for their own purposes: the Nationalists thought they could share power with Hitler; industrialists thought the Nazis would defend them against trade unions and Communists, so they gave Hitler money; army officers thought the Nazis would give the army back its important place in Germany.

D Magazine cover 1932. The German words say: 'The meaning of the Hitler salute. Millions stand behind me. Little man asks for great gifts.'

All of these people thought they could control Hitler in government. A former Chancellor, Franz von Papen, persuaded President Hindenburg to make Hitler leader of a coalition government with only two other Nazis. On 30 January 1933 Hitler became Chancellor of Germany.

Investigating

As part of your assessment, you will have to carry out a historical investigation. This exercise will help you to practise the skills you need to do it well. There are three stages in investigating:

1 planning
- deciding what you are going to find out about.
- setting yourself questions to answer.
- finding sources of information.

2 recording
- choosing information from your sources that will help to answer your questions.
- writing the information under suitable sub-headings.

3 presenting
- writing a report on what you have found out.
- answering the questions you set yourself.
- coming to a conclusion.

Starting Point

By 1928 it looked as though the Nazis might be finished. Only twelve Nazis were elected to the Reichstag in that year.

In July 1932 230 Nazis won seats in the Reichstag. On 30 January 1933 their leader, Adolf Hitler, became Chancellor of Germany.

Planning

1. The first stage is to work out a purpose for your investigation.

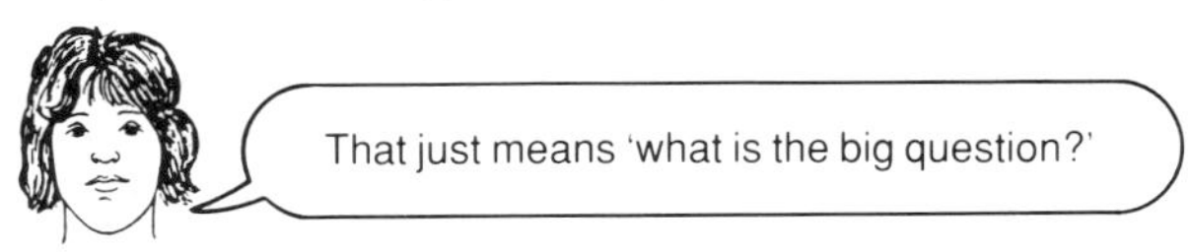

Now look at the starting point above. What do you think is the big question to ask about the events described there? Write your answer at the top of the planning sheet. A planning sheet is on page 47. This will give you your title.
If you find it hard to make up a big question, remember that historians are always asking 'Why?'

2. Now you need three or four smaller questions that will help you to answer the big one.
On the planning sheet you will find one possible question. Under it, write at least two more questions that you think will help.

3. You will now have to choose your sources. These can be of two kinds:
Primary Sources are ones written or made at the time you are studying. They may include letters, newspapers, photographs, memoirs or even recorded interviews.
Secondary Sources are books, articles, pictures or programmes made by people living later: by historians, teachers, you and me. Your report will be a secondary source.

In this book I have used primary and secondary sources. For this investigation you may use these. I suggest you begin with the ones in this chapter. You should also use any books or other sources your teacher can lend you, and visit your school and public libraries.

Recording

People who study and write about history always have to make choices. They cannot write *everything* down, so they have to choose what is most important to record.
When reading your sources, you must decide which information in them helps to answer your questions. You must *organise* your notes.
You will have a record sheet for each of your small questions. A model for a record sheet for you to copy is on page 47. At the top of each write one of these questions. That way you won't muddle which information goes with which question. As far as possible you should make notes in your own words. For each piece of information you write down, keep a note of where you found it in the right column.

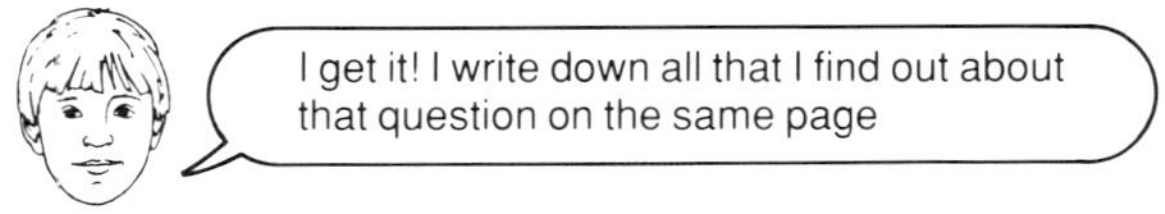

Presenting

You now have to write a report showing what you have found out. In it, you must do <u>two</u> things:

1. Answer each of your small questions.

2. Draw a conclusion about your big question. You will have to support your conclusion by giving your reasons for reaching it.

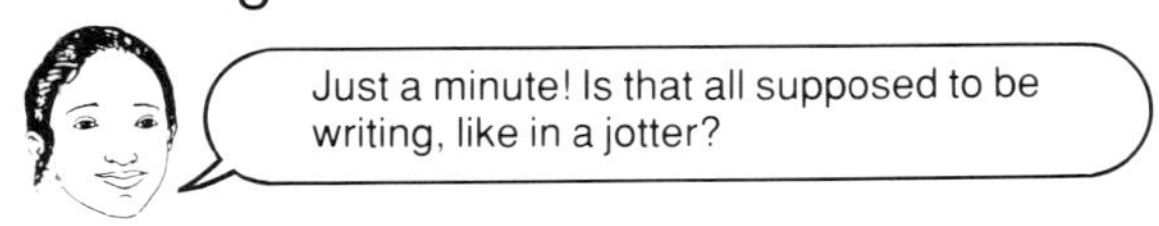

Certainly not. Your report may take several forms. For example:

- it may be written up like a booklet
- it may be made up as a wallchart
- it may be recorded onto tape.

It need not all be writing. Diagrams, pictures and other illustrations may be very useful.
You should discuss with your teacher what kind of report will help you to show off your work best.

Group discussion

Once the investigations have been completed, each person in your group should make a report to the other members of the group. You will find that people have reached different conclusions about why Hitler was able to reach power.

Make a list of about six factors that the members of your group think helped Hitler to become Chancellor. Using this list as a basis, discuss which of the factors your group thinks were most important. Make sure you use the evidence you have gathered to support your point of view. At the end your group should vote to put the factors in order of importance.

Planning sheet

1. The Big Question – The Title

What do you think is most important to explain about the events described in the box on page 45?

Write your answer here ______

2. The Small Questions – The Sub-Headings

Here is one question that will have to be answered, in order to answer the big question:

1) What happened in Germany to make people listen to the Nazis again?

Now write down TWO or THREE other questions that you think are important.

2) ______

3) ______

4) ______

Only if you get really stuck should you ask your teacher for help.

Record Sheet Name:

Subject/Question:

Source	*Evidence*
Author	
Title	
Type	
Page	

11 THE NAZI REVOLUTION

The Reichstag Fire

Hitler was Chancellor, but did not yet have full power. Only two other Nazis were in the government. Even with the Nationalists, he did not have a majority in the Reichstag. He called an election for March, hoping to get enough seats to do what he liked.

One week before the election, Hitler was at dinner with Goebbels when dramatic news reached him.

A Suddenly a 'phone call from Dr. Hanfstaengl: 'The Reichstag is on Fire!' I take this for a piece of wild fantasy and refuse to report it to the Leader. I ask for news wherever possible and at last obtain the dreadful confirmation: it is true! . . . I immediately inform the Leader and we hasten at top speed . . . to the Reichstag. The whole building is aflame . . . There is no doubt but that Communism has made a last attempt to cause disorder by means of fear and terror, in order to grasp power during the general panic.

Dr Josef Goebbels' diary, 27 February 1933.

B The Reichstag building on fire. Only some parts of the building were damaged badly.

A young Dutchman called Marinus van der Lubbe was found in the building. He had taken off his shirt and set it alight. Then he had run through the building using it to set fire to old furniture and curtains. His claim to be a Communist was all Hitler needed as an excuse to act. Out of control with excitement, he yelled,

C Every Communist official must be shot. All Communist deputies must be hanged this very night. All friends of the Communists must be locked up.

Hitler's orders given at the burning Reichstag.

At once Hitler asked President Hindenburg for special powers. He got them. The fundamental laws in the Constitution (see chapter 4) were suspended. Many Communists were arrested, as the Nazis claimed they had planned a revolution. Hitler hoped that fear of Communism would make many Germans vote for his party in the elections.

As for van der Lubbe, although even the police chief thought he was crazy, he was tried and executed.

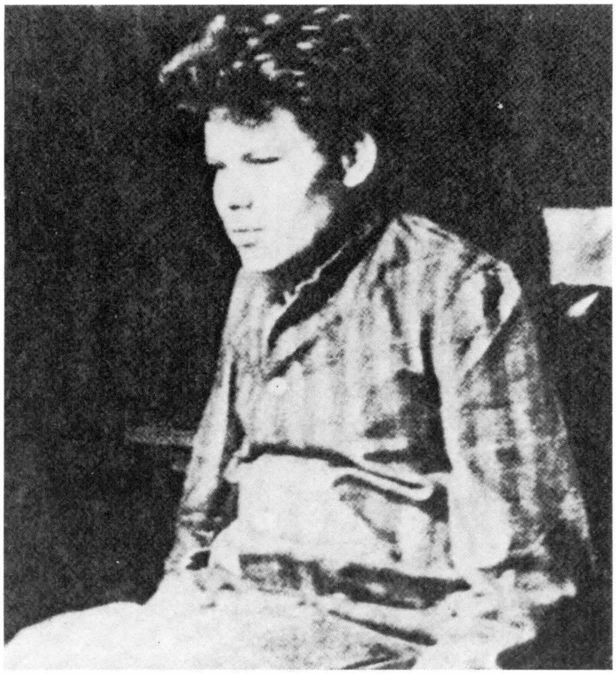

D Photograph of van der Lubbe, taken at his trial.

?

1. Why did Hitler want another election in March 1933?
2. Why was the Reichstag fire useful to Hitler, coming only a week before the election was to be held?
3. What use did Hitler make of the fire?
4. In source A, what evidence is there that the Nazi leaders were taken by surprise by the news of the fire?
5. What was Hitler's reaction to the fire?

Imaginative reconstruction
Using the information in the text and sources, write a report on the fire as though you were reporting it for a radio news programme. You should describe what has happened, comment on the reaction of people who are present, and say what you think will happen next.

Role play

The class should divide into groups, representing political parties as follows: Communist Party (KPD)
Social Democratic Party (SPD)
Centre Party (ZENTRUM)
German National People's Party (DNVP)
National Socialist German Workers' Party (NSDAP)

Preparation

In your group, use the information you have learned in the course so far to make up two lists:

- arguments in favour of your own party, explaining its main ideas and strengths.
- arguments against the parties you see as your main enemies. Use these to prepare an election address on behalf of your party.

The Meeting

One person from each group reads the party's election address to the class. There is then a question session, when members of each group can challenge the others on points made in their speeches.
If you wish, a vote can then be taken. In this vote, groups may not vote for their own party.

TERROR AGAINST THE REDS

Almost as soon as news of the Reichstag fire spread, there were stories that the Nazis had started it themselves. It seemed just too convenient for them, especially with van der Lubbe's claim to be a member of the Dutch Communist Party. The German Communist Party at once made enquiries in Holland.

D We immediately telegraphed our sister party in Holland, and we can confirm that the accused . . . is completely unknown, and has never belonged to the Communist Party.

Special edition of Communist newspaper, 28 February 1933.

Most historians now accept that the fire was, in fact, the work of van der Lubbe. The speed of the Nazis in exploiting their opportunity was remarkable, however. The day after the fire President Hindenburg issued a decree under Article 48 of the Constitution (see source H, chapter 4, p.22).

E Restrictions on personal liberty, on the right of free expression of opinion, including freedom of the press, on the right of assembly . . . and violations on the privacy of postal . . . and telephone communications . . ., are allowed beyond the legal limits otherwise set out.

Decree for the Protection of People and State, 28 February 1933.

The Nazis did not even wait for the decree. During the night they used the S.A. as extra police to drag the Communists from their homes, and raided Karl Liebknecht House, the Communist Party headquarters. Nearly 5,000 people were arrested.

To justify their actions, the government announced that their raid on Karl Liebknecht House had uncovered plans for a Communist campaign of terror including arson attacks, the kidnapping of the families of police officers for use as human shields, and torture of opponents. In reply, the Communists claimed the entire exercise was prepared in advance against themselves and the whole working class. Such actions would make Nazi success in the elections more certain.

THE MARCH ELECTION

In the last week before the elections the Nazis were in evidence everywhere. Parades, demonstrations, flags and loudspeakers spread their message, while the S.A. intimidated their opponents, tore down their posters and replaced these with Nazi ones. Hitler was clever enough not to outlaw the Communist Party yet, so that the workers' votes would not all go to the Social Democrats.

With all this pressure, the election result was amazing. The Nazis did increase their vote, and became the largest single party with 288 seats. But they did not gain a majority; 56 per cent of Germans voted against them.

F S.A. man acting as auxiliary policeman guards Communist prisoners.

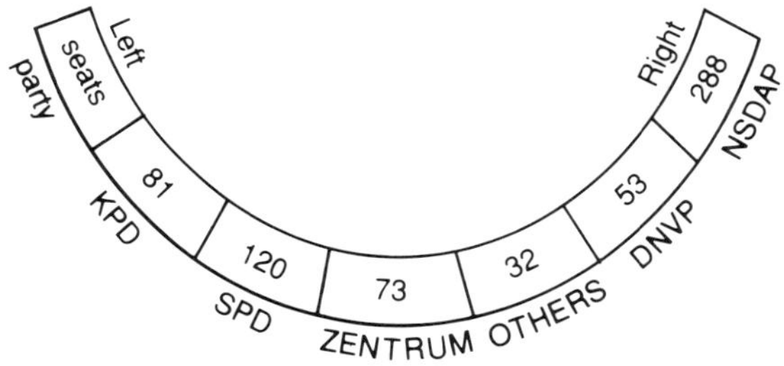

G Reichstag Election Results – March 1933.

THE ENABLING LAW

The members of the Reichstag met in Berlin's Kroll Opera House. The Nazis had set the scene to make the greatest impact possible. A huge swastika banner covered the wall behind the government seats. The National Socialist deputies, dressed in S.A. uniforms, welcomed Hitler with arms stretched out in salute. The deputies from other parties had to pass through lines of S.S. men outside the building and S.A. men in every corridor. The atmosphere was intimidating.

At once, Hitler demanded a new law to give him even more power. Hitler needed a two-thirds majority to pass the law he wanted. Partly from fear, and partly because Hitler promised to respect the rights of the Roman Catholic Church, the Zentrum voted for the law. The Communists were not allowed in, so this vote was decisive. Only 94 brave Social Democrats voted against.

H Article 1. In addition to the procedure for passing laws outlined in the Constitution, the Reich Cabinet is authorised to make laws . . .
Article 2. The laws enacted by the Reich Cabinet may deviate from the Constitution . . .
Article 3. The national laws enacted by the Reich Cabinet shall be prepared by the Chancellor and published . . .

Enabling Law, 24 March 1933.

When Hermann Göring announced the result, the Nazis rose as one to roar their approval. Giving the Nazi salute, they sang the Horst Wessel song, their party's theme tune. Their triumph was echoed by cheering crowds outside.

I The street gangs had seized control of the resources of a great modern state, the gutter had come to power.

Alan Bullock, Hitler: A Study in Tyranny, *1962.*

In effect, Hitler could now do as he pleased. Other political parties gradually vanished. In June the government banned the SPD. With no real parliament, the Democrats, Nationalists and Zentrum found they had no purpose left, so dissolved themselves. In July a new law stated that the Nazi Party was the only party in Germany. It became a criminal offence to form another party. In only six months, the Nazis had destroyed all trace of democratic government in Germany.

?

1 a Why do you think the German Communists sent a telegram to the Dutch Communists? (Source D.)
  b Why would they have been so anxious to show that van der Lubbe was not a genuine Communist?
2 How did the Nazis use the Reichstag fire to reinforce their power? (Sources E and F.)
3 Use your knowledge and the sources to describe and explain the results of the election of March 1933.
4 What was the effect of the Enabling Law? (Source H.) Why might it be seen as marking the end of democracy in Germany?
5 Do you accept the view that the events of January–July 1933 show that including Article 48 in the Weimar Constitution (source H, chapter 4, p.22), was a mistake that proved fatal for democracy in Germany? Explain your answer fully.

12 DER FÜHRER

● *Dictatorship*

On 2 August 1934 President Hindenburg died. At once, Adolf Hitler became President as well as Chancellor. He was to be known as Der Führer – the Leader. He was also Commander-in-Chief of the Armed Forces. At last he had complete power over Germany.

Governments treat their people in different ways. Some are fair and kind, but others are harsh and cruel. The way they work depends on what they want to do.

The men who started the Weimar Republic wanted all Germans to have a say in government. They gave each adult a vote. They wanted Germans to be free, so they gave each person rights. (You will find them in source C, chapter 4, p.20).

Hitler's Nazis wanted to keep power for themselves. The S.A. and the new secret police, the Gestapo, arrested people who might oppose the government. They were sent to the first concentration camps in Germany.

It was dangerous to speak against the Nazis, even in private. Spies were everywhere. People were encouraged to report friends, neighbours, even relations who said the wrong thing. When one person vanished during the night it was easy for others to keep quiet.

To strengthen Germany, the Nazis wanted to create a 'pure' German people – a 'master race'. This meant getting rid of everyone they did not want. Cripples and the mentally ill were not fit enough for the new Germany. Others were not seen as real Germans. This applied to the Jews especially. People like these suffered dreadfully under the Nazis. (See chapter 13.)

A Communists are arrested in Berlin, 1933.

● *The Leader*

Hitler's government was cruel. It hurt or frightened many Germans. Yet Hitler himself was very popular. He tried to appear as someone who really cared for his people.

B Hitler visits a factory in 1935. The caption in the magazine said, 'Bond with the workers'.

C Hitler meets a young apprentice at the same factory.

Even when people dared to complain about Nazi rule, they blamed his followers, not Hitler himself. 'If the Führer knew about it . . .', they would say, believing he would sort out the problems.

D A specially posed propaganda shot of Hitler. Note the admiration on the faces of the young people.

?

1 What decides how a government treats its people?

2 Copy this table and complete it by saying which right in source C, chapter 4, p.20, matches each reason.

	Right	This was important because
1.		it let people protest if something was wrong.
2.		it stopped the government from locking up people they didn't like.
3.		it let people speak against the government.

3 Use the text and source A to say what the Nazis did to take away each of these rights.

4 Sources B and C both come from a Nazi magazine. What do you think each one was meant to show about Hitler?

*H*ITLER'S GOVERNMENT

In Hitler's first months in power the only other Nazis in his Cabinet were Wilhelm Frick as Minister of the Interior and Hermann Göring, whose main responsibilities were in the Prussian state government. The Nationalists and other conservatives who shared power with the Nazis expected to control them. They were taken aback by the pace at which the Nazis moved.

Göring's position let him replace many senior civil servants, including police officers, with Nazis. He issued orders to the police to oppose socialist or communist organisations, but to support nationalist groups. He even enlisted 40,000 S.A. and S.S. men as auxiliary policemen. This made it easy to squash their opponents after the Reichstag fire.

By the end of June 1933 the other members of the coalition, except for Vice-Chancellor von Papen, had been replaced by Nazis. With the elimination of other political parties by July, it seemed that the Nazi revolution was complete.

*T*HE NIGHT OF THE LONG KNIVES

Hitler's main problem now lay within the party. Having helped him to reach power, Ernst Röhm's S.A. was now a liability. Röhm wanted his S.A. to become the core of a new German army into which the existing army would be absorbed. More importantly, he demanded that the revolution should not end, but change direction.

D Anyone who wanted to be a fellow-traveller only during shining torchlight processions and impressive parades . . . and now believes he has taken part in the German revolution – can go home! He has confused the 'national uprising' with the German revolution! . . . If bourgeois simpletons think it is enough that the State . . . has received a new sign, that the 'national' revolution has already lasted too long, for once we agree with them. It is in fact high time the national revolution stopped and became the National Socialist one.

Ernst Röhm, June 1933.

This kind of talk worried Hitler. He needed a period of stability to gain the confidence of the army, the civil service and German business. If they feared a social revolution they could still act together to overthrow him.

Röhm's enemies in the NSDAP, led by Göring and S.S. leader Heinrich Himmler, persuaded Hitler that Röhm was planning to use the S.A. to seize power himself. The Führer decided to act.

On 30 June 1934 Hitler went to Wiessee, a resort in Bavaria, where the S.A. leaders were meeting. Supported by S.S. men, he arrested Röhm personally while others rounded up the remaining S.A. officers. They were taken to Stadelheim Prison in Münich. Two S.S. men were taken to Röhm's cell.

E There they handed over a Browning to Röhm, who . . . asked to speak to Hitler. They ordered him to shoot himself. If he did not comply, they would come back in ten minutes and kill him . . . When the time was up, the two S.S. men re-entered the cell, and found Röhm standing with his chest bared. Immediately one of them from the door shot him in the throat.

Account by the prison governor.

In Berlin, Münich and other cities S.A. leaders were murdered along with others who had incurred Nazi anger. In total, it is likely that over 400 people were killed, including former Nazi leader Gregor Strasser, army General Schleicher and the retired Bavarian leader, von Kahr.

F A contemporary cartoon from Czechoslovakia.

THEY SALUTE WITH BOTH HANDS NOW

G Low's famous comment on the executions. Göring is on Hitler's right, while Goebbels crouches behind him. Soldiers of the army stand with bayonets fixed.

Two weeks later, Hitler spoke to the Reichstag. After accusing the S.A. leaders of corruption and revolutionary ambition, he defended his own actions.

H If anyone . . . asks why I did not resort to the regular courts of justice, then all I can say to him is this: in this hour I was responsible for the fate of the German people, and thereby I became the supreme judge of the German people.

Hitler's speech, 13 July 1934.

The message to other possible opponents was clear.

?

1 Using the information in chapters 11 and 12, make a list of the reasons why the Nazis were able to take complete control of Germany so quickly in 1933. Choose which you think was the most important reason, and explain your choice.

2 What evidence is there in source D that Röhm did not think the Nazis had achieved all of their aims by gaining power? Which people in Germany might have been alarmed by this statement?

3 Describe how Hitler rid himself of the danger to his rule presented by the S.A. What justification did he give in source H for his actions?

Source analysis

4 What different views of Hitler and his actions are shown in sources F and G? Explain in detail how each artist has created the impression he wanted.

5 Which of these interpretations do you think is the more accurate? Explain your answer.

6 What value do these cartoons have for historians trying to understand the period?

Co-ordination

Nazi rule meant the close supervision of all aspects of life. Germans were encouraged to adopt a Nazi outlook. Those who would not be encouraged were terrorised into doing so, at least in public.

The party had representatives everywhere, from the block wardens who watched the inhabitants of a street to the S.S. men used as labour police on the factory floor.

I The lives of us all are continually threatened, and we are under observation all the time . . . They keep a record of every one of us on a card index, and on it they write whether we give anything for the Winter Help*, whether we put out flags, how big the flags are, and how we hang them . . . I have never occupied myself with politics . . . but suddenly everything has become political, whatever I say or do, or whatever I don't say or don't do.

Letter from a young German worker, January 1939.

*Winter Help – a fund that was supposed to give relief to the poor, but was often used for party purposes.

Hitler was clear about his purpose. In 1933 he told a meeting of generals that the public had to learn to think as a nation, so that Germany's strength could be restored. This helps to explain the censorship which tried to destroy anything that did not fit the Nazi version of German nationality.

The nation was to be welded together by a process of 'Co-ordination'. Opponents had to be silenced while organisations from the churches to sports clubs had to take on a suitably German identity.

Trade Unions were dangerous because they might give the workers an alternative loyalty. They were made illegal, their leaders were jailed, and they were replaced by the Labour Front. Under the leadership of Robert Ley, it pretended to represent the workers, but its real function was to give Germany a disciplined work-force. Other possible centres of opposition suffered too. Within a year, half of the teaching staff at Düsseldorf University and a third of those in Berlin and Frankfurt had been dismissed.

J S.A. men collect 'un-German' books for burning. The poster on the lorry reads 'German students march against the un-German spirit'.

CONCENTRATION CAMPS

The concentration camps were not reserved for the Jews. Anyone who was inconvenient for the Nazis: politicians, union leaders, the mentally ill or physically crippled, could be sent there. These camps were run according to tough rules.

K Reporting sick without reason – penalty, 5 days' confinement to cells and several weeks of hard labour.
Making disrespectful . . . remarks about an S.S. man or deliberately failing to salute – penalty, 8 days' confinement to cells, 25 strokes of the birch at the beginning of the period and another 25 at the end.
Talking politics, making speeches . . . collecting true or untrue information about the concentration camps . . . penalty, those committing these offences will be hanged.

From the rules of Lichtenburg concentration camp.

Many millions of people suffered terribly in the camps. Their hair was shaved off and they were forced to wear prison uniforms. They had to work very hard, with very little food. At Buchenwald alone, over 33,000 people died in eight years, one in every seven of those who were sent there.

The cruelty of the camps and the air of menace brought about by sudden arrests and the constant presence of the S.S. and Gestapo frightened many ordinary Germans into acceptance of Nazi rule, or at least an unwillingness to oppose it openly.

L 'As in the Middle Ages, so in the Third Reich.' In this photomontage a German artist shows the swastika as a modern weapon of torture like the medieval wheel.

?

1 a. What evidence in source I shows that ordinary Germans believed they were being watched constantly?
b. Think of the practical problems in gathering and using such information. How justified do you think the views expressed in source I were?
c. Even if these beliefs were exaggerated, what does the source tell you about life in Nazi Germany?

2 Using the sources and your knowledge, describe how the Nazis kept the people of Germany under control. Your answer should take the form of a short essay of several paragraphs.

13 'THE MASTER RACE'

The Jews

When Hitler was a boy many people in Germany and other countries disliked the Jews. This hatred of Jews is called anti-Semitism. It happened for several reasons.

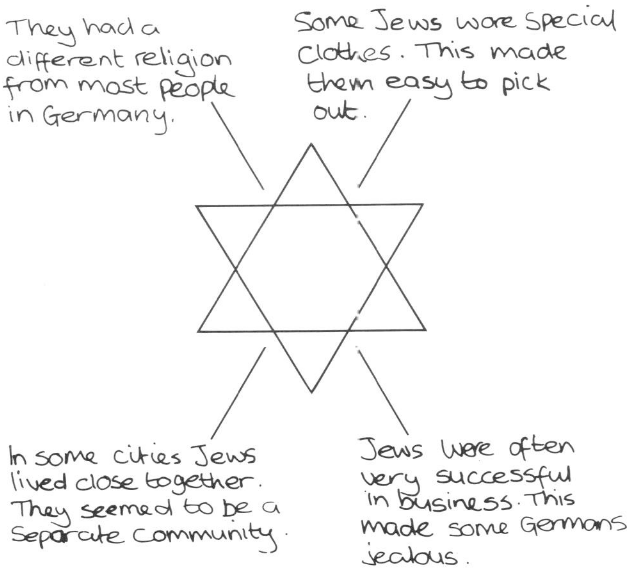

Hitler first became aware of Jews while in Vienna.

A One day, when passing through the Inner City of Vienna, I suddenly saw a creature in a long caftan [robe]. My first thought was: is this a Jew? I watched the man secretly, but the longer I gazed, the more the question shaped itself in my brain: is this a German?

Adolf Hitler, Mein Kampf.

The Nazis blamed the Jews for Germany's problems after the war. They said that the Jews were Communists and that Jewish greed was ruining the German economy. These two statements did not make sense. If one were true, the other was false. This did not bother the Nazis. They intended only to give the German people a target for their anger.

B Poster for a film called 'The Eternal Jew', 1937. The hammer and sickle of Communism are on a map of Germany, and the coins suggest money lending. The drawing of the Jew is a caricature of what the Nazis said Jews looked like.

Cruelty

Once in power, the Nazis acted against the Jews. Jewish doctors, lawyers and civil servants were sacked. Germans were asked not to use Jewish shops.

C S.A. man supports a boycott of Jewish shops in April 1933.

Teachers and pupils made fun of Jewish children in schools. Many Jews were arrested and sent to concentration camps.

Then in 1938 a young Jew murdered a German official in Paris. This was used as an excuse to attack Jews living in Germany. Hundreds of houses and shops were destroyed, and 20,000 Jews arrested. Young Karl Hartland lived in Essen. His father took him to see the remains of the synagogue which had been set on fire.

D The front gate was closed and smoke was coming out of the roof . . . Smoke came out of the top windows and the windows in the room where Karl had had his religious instruction lessons were broken. There was no sign of the fire brigade and a small group of storm troopers stood there looking as if all this had nothing to do with them.

Charles Hannam, A Boy in Your Situation, *1977.*

?

Group discussion

Keep a record of your group's decisions. One of the group should report back to the class at the end.

- For what reasons were the Jews unpopular in Germany?
- What evidence is there in the sources that the Nazi government encouraged Germans to hurt Jewish people?
- If you had been an ordinary German, how would you have felt about living under a government that acted this way?

*R*ACISM

The Nazis gloried in being racists. In their programme in 1920 source D, chapter 5, pages 25–26 they had declared that only those of German blood should be allowed to be members of the nation. Their ideas of racial character and superiority went much further. Germans were told they were Aryans, a pure breed of high quality destined to rule over lesser peoples like Slavs, Jews and blacks. To maintain their superiority, they had to maintain the purity of the race.

E It is never by war that nations are ruined, but by the loss of their powers of resistance, which are exclusively a characteristic of pure racial blood. In this world everything that is not of sound stock is like chaff.

Adolf Hitler, Mein Kampf.

These teachings were popular. It was comforting for Germans, suffering from humiliation and poverty, to be told they would be a 'master race', commanding respect throughout the world. It was also convenient to blame your troubles on those 'foreigners', the Jews.

Once in power, the Nazis set about creating what they called the 'national community'. Those of Aryan blood – the 'national comrades' – were portrayed as healthy, handsome and purposeful; lesser breeds – the 'community aliens' – were shown as weak in mind and body.

*T*REATMENT OF THE JEWS

To protect the Aryan race from contamination by Jews, the Nuremberg Laws were passed in 1935. Already discriminated against, now the Jews were denied their identity as Germans.

G Marriages between Jews and nationals of German or similar blood are forbidden. A Jew may not be a citizen of the Reich. He has no vote in political matters; he may not fill public office.

From the Nuremberg Laws, 1935.

These laws defined precisely those who were to be regarded as Jews, and banned Jews from employing German women of child-bearing age as house servants. 'Aryan' Germans were encouraged to break off all contacts with Jews. The British wife of a German lawyer did not realise their effects at first.

'National Comrades'

'Community aliens'

F Pictures from a Biology textbook.

H The Nuremberg Laws did not hit me hard until they walked quietly and with dignity across the threshold of my own front door. Professor Bauer looked after our children . . . I was a little puzzled, and very grateful, that he found time one night to sit with me . . . while Nicholas, our eldest son, tossed with fever . . .

Professor Bauer hesitated before leaving the house and then asked me quietly if . . . I still wished for him to attend my family. Still? Why ever not? . . . I knew, doubtless, that he was a Jew. I might not have heard, though, that his Clinic had been threatened with having to close down unless he handed it over to an Aryan colleague . . . He had received threatening letters bidding him to keep his hands off Aryan children. If I insisted I might get involved.

Christabel Bielenberg, The Past is Myself, *1984.*

Soon, Jews had to mark themselves by wearing yellow stars. Then, in 1937, Jewish men and women whose first names were not obviously Jewish had to add Israel or Sara to them.

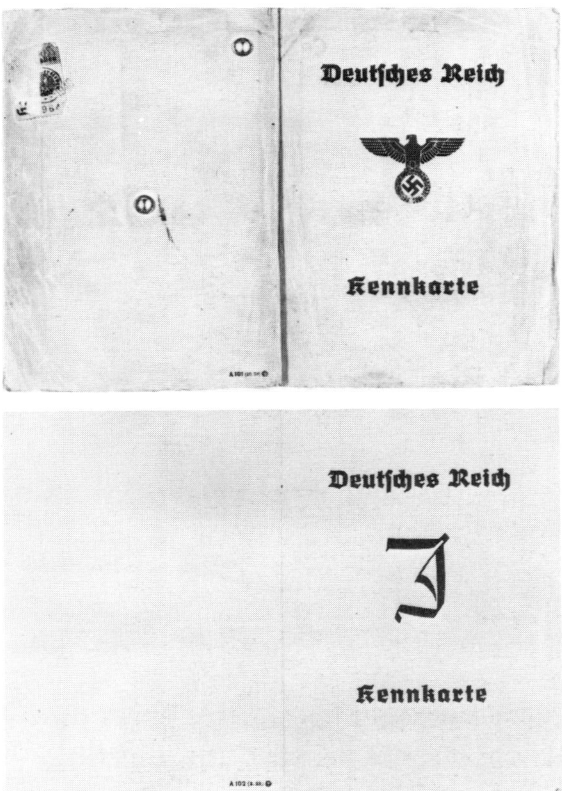

I Covers of identity cards from Nazi Germany. Above is a normal one, and below a Jewish one.

At first many Jews, unwilling to believe the persecution could last, tried to live out the trouble. Only the violence of 1938 and the concentration camps made them flee.

WHAT PEOPLE THOUGHT

Most ordinary Germans were not strongly anti-Semitic. They did not take much part in the oppression, though they did little to prevent it or protest against it, except when there was violence. Even then they dared not do too much, for fear of what might happen to them.

J The brutal measures against the Jews have caused great indignation among the population. People spoke their minds quite openly, and many Aryans were arrested as a result . . . Many people are looking after the Jewish women and children and have put them up in their homes. Housewives are shopping for the Jewish women, because it is forbidden to sell food to them.

Report from Germany, November 1938.

K Some have welcomed the actions taken against the Jews; others watched them calmly; others again are sorry for the Jews, though they do not necessarily express this openly.

Police report, 26 November 1938.

?

1. How did the Nazis try to justify their treatment of Jews and other groups? (Sources A,B,E, and F.)
2. In what ways were Jewish people persecuted? (Sources C,D,G,H, and I.)
3. Do sources H,J, and K agree about the attitude of ordinary Germans towards the treatment of the Jews? Explain your answer.

Group discussion

Why were the Nazis able to get away with their racist policies? What does your study of this issue tell you about the values current in Germany in the 1930s?

14 LIFE UNDER HITLER

● *The Nuremberg Rallies*

The Nazis attracted many young men with the glamour of uniforms and parades. These were shown off best in the Party Day rallies in the city of Nuremberg. The first one took place in 1925. Only two years later 20,000 people marched through the city streets to listen to Hitler speak.

As Führer, Hitler used these annual rallies to impress the people of Germany, and the rest of the world. A young architect, Albert Speer, designed a massive new stadium for the 1934 rally.

Overlooking the stadium was a huge stone eagle, its wingspan over 30 metres across. The arena was surrounded by hundreds of long, red banners each with the black swastika against a white circle in the middle.

Party members came from all over Germany. There were rehearsals to make sure all would go smoothly. On 7 September marching bands led a procession of uniformed S.A. and S.S. men, with flags flying and standards held high, to the floodlit stadium. Over 200,000 of them stood in straight lines. First, party leaders like Rudolf Hess excited them, with fiery speeches and slogans.

A Hitler at the 1934 rally.

B The party is Hitler. Hitler is Germany just as Germany is Hitler. Heil Hitler!

From a speech by Rudolf Hess at Nuremberg, 1934.

Then Hitler's voice reached them through the loudspeakers. When he told them, 'We are strong and will get stronger!' they roared back '*Sieg Heil!*' – Hail Victory!, their arms straight in salute.

The great floodlight meeting was the climax of days of processions, meetings and displays. The displays showed how Hitler was keeping his promise to rebuild the army so that Germany could be great once more.

C Tanks and infantry take part in a mock battle at the 1938 rally.

Rallies like these gave the German people excitement and a feeling of belonging. Those who could not be there heard the speeches on the radio or watched the newsreel film in the cinema. They could share in the atmosphere, and feel proud to hear their national anthem again.

?

1 Copy these sentences into your notebook. Use sources A and C to help you fill in the blanks. The Nuremberg rallies showed that the army was important in Nazi Germany. Two things that show this are:

____

and ____________________ .

2 Choose from these statements the one you think best explains what Rudolf Hess meant in source B. Give a reason for your choice.

- Hitler is the ruler of Germany.
- Hitler and the German people want the same things.
- Hitler is like any ordinary German.

3 What do you think was the purpose of holding rallies like these?

MILITARISM

The Nuremberg rallies provide only one example of how the Nazis gave every part of German life a military look. Discipline was central to the regime, even if it had to be imposed by fear. Organisations used military style uniforms. Almost every month in the year had its festival, complete with military parades. For example, on 30 January there was a celebration of the anniversary of Hitler's becoming Chancellor, 1 May saw the 'Day of Labour' and on 9 November the 'old fighters' marched through Munich to recall the failed rising of 1923. At every excuse, there was a march past, a torchlight procession or a military display.

The emphasis on military display was matched by a growth in military strength. Hitler completely ignored the military clauses of Versailles. The army of 100,000 men had become 550,000 by 1936 and 850,000 by 1938, with a further 900,000 trained reserves.

D Motorised parade as Hitler opens a section of the autobahn between Frankfurt and Heidelberg.

E S.S. men on parade at Nuremberg, 1935.

F

German Military Spending 1933-39 (in millions of Reichsmarks)

1933	1,900	1937	8,200
1934	1,900	1938	18,400
1935	4,000	1939	32,300
1936	5,800		

Here, at least, Hitler was keeping his promises. With a new navy, air force and armoured land forces, he had made Germany strong enough to take the risk of sending troops into the Rhineland in 1936. The failure of Britain and France to resist encouraged him to be even more aggressive in the future.

EMPLOYMENT

The growth of the armed forces helped Hitler to keep another of his promises. Unemployment in Germany fell rapidly as men joined the forces, built tanks, ships and aircraft, or took part in the programme of public works which covered Germany with autobahns, stadia and new government buildings. The unemployment figures were also brought down by the flight of Jews abroad and by the imprisonment of many in the concentration camps. Yet the figures remain dramatic.

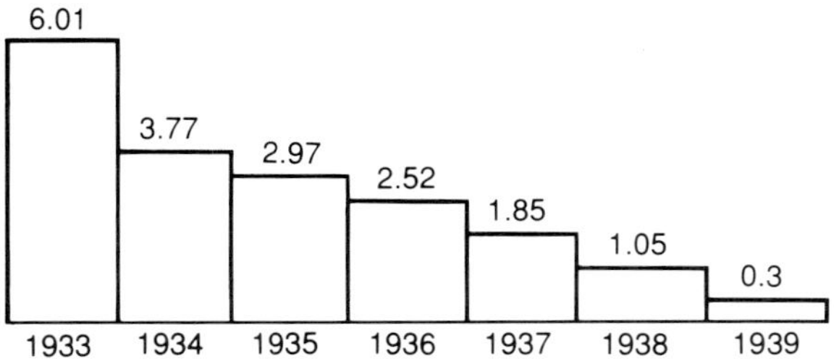

G Unemployment in Germany 1933-1939 (in millions).

By 1939 Germany's greatest economic problem was a serious shortage of skilled labour.

'Bread and circuses'

It was critical to Hitler that his drive to strengthen Germany should not be ruined by strikes or other labour troubles. Strikes were illegal, and the replacement of the unions by the German Labour Front made united action unlikely. Still, to prevent troubles in industry, the Nazis felt it necessary to give the workers some sense of well-being.

Wages were generally slightly higher than they had been under the Weimar Republic, but not enough to guarantee contentment. A special section of the Labour Front was set up to offer encouragement and reward to the workers. 'Strength through Joy' offered subsidised package holidays and organised theatre visits, held sports courses and ran outdoor activities. These events become very popular.

H Almost all national comrades rate Strength through Joy as one of National Socialism's really creditable achievements . . .

I attended a swimming course in which over 50 took part, and I have to admit there was very little party atmosphere. The participants were all ordinary people. There were scarcely any 'Heil Hitlers'. Coming from the old workers' sports clubs as we did, we felt at home, so to speak . . .

It is pretty generally the case now that you can't avoid Strength through Joy if you want to travel or take part in sport . . . There is simply no other choice.

Report to the Social Democratic Party in Exile, 1936.

As well as occupying people's spare time, the Nazis tried to offer them an incentive to work hard. They could join a savings scheme, which would give them the chance to own their own 'People's Car', the Volkswagen, which appeared in 1938. In fact, the scheme did not work very well, and few ordinary Germans claimed their car.

The ultimate public show was the staging of the Olympic Games in Berlin in 1936. Germany prepared to welcome thousands of overseas visitors, and to show them how good life was under National Socialism. Even anti-Jewish posters were removed while the Games were on. Over 100,000 spectators watched the opening ceremony, in which girls dressed in white danced, and boys with coloured tunics formed the Olympic rings, while bands played Beethoven's 'Ode to Joy'. Despite Hitler's failure to congratulate black athletes who won medals, the Games were tremendously successful as a publicity exercise.

I 'Olympic guests – quick march.' A photomontage by John Heartfield. Dr. Goebbels is holding the strings.

1. What evidence is there in sources A, D and E of the importance of military discipline and symbols in the life of Nazi Germany?
2. In what other ways did militarism show itself in Hitler's Germany?
3. a. Was the author of source H a Nazi supporter? Give at least two reasons for your answer.
   b. Why is source H useful as evidence of the treatment of ordinary people in Germany?
4. What use does the artist in source I believe the Nazis were making of the Olympic Games? Explain your answer.

K Advertisement – 'All Germany hears the Führer on the People's Receiver.'

PROPAGANDA

As John Heartfield's montage suggests, the Nazis used the Olympic Games as an exercise in international propaganda. At home, the German people were subjected to constant doses of the same medicine.

The parades, the bands, the flags were part of this campaign, but it went much further. From 1933, Dr Goebbels was head of the new Ministry for Public Information and Propaganda. He was well aware of the power of the mass media. Films and newspapers, theatres and radio, magazines and art galleries were all subject to his censorship. The messages they carried all had to reflect the beliefs and values of the Party. The purpose of communication was to carry these beliefs to every German.

J Through technical devices like the radio and the loud-speaker, eighty million people were deprived of independent thought. It was thereby possible to subject them all to the will of one man.

Albert Speer's final speech at his trial at Nuremberg, 1946.

After 1933 the propaganda message changed. Now the main concerns were to convince the 'national comrades' of the virtues of living in the National Socialist state, and to persuade them to participate in the activities of the 'national community'.

Economic successes were advertised, along with the virtues of hard work and service. There were successes to celebrate. Not only did unemployment fall, but industrial production increased by 45 per cent in the first two years of Nazi rule and by another 45 per cent in the next three years. Germans were also pleased by the return to Germany of the Saar after a plebiscite in 1935 and the reoccupation of the Rhineland in 1936.

Hitler claimed to have begun a new social order.

L By my side stand Germans from all walks of life who today are amongst the leaders of the nation: men who once were workers on the land are now governing German states . . . It is true that men who came from the bourgeoisie and former aristocrats have their place in this Movement.

But to us it matters nothing whence they came if only they can work to the profit of our people . . . We have not broken down classes in order to set new ones in their place: we have broken down classes to make way for the German people as a whole.

Hitler speaking in Berlin, 1 May 1937.

At every opportunity examples were shown of people sharing the new national spirit.

M A 1938 magazine shows how workers spent their breaks 'before' and 'after' 1933.

WOMEN IN THE THIRD REICH

One way in which male unemployment was reduced was by encouraging women to give up work. The Nazis posed as having a chivalrous attitude towards women, but in practice this high talk was camouflage for a policy of male domination. As usual, Hitler dressed this up in fancy phrases and flattery.

N If one says that man's world is the State . . . one might be tempted to say that the world of woman is a smaller world. For her world is her husband, her family, her children and her house. But where would the greater world be if there were no one to care for the smaller world?

Hitler speaking at the 1934 Nuremberg rally.

Put more crudely, women ought to stick to the three Ks: *Kinder*, *Kirche*, *Küche* – Kids, Kirk, Kitchen.

Women were offered rewards for conforming to this model. Couples getting married could get state loans, but only if the wife gave up her job in a factory or office. An Aryan woman who had four or more children was awarded a medal, the Cross of Motherhood.

In practice, it was impossible for German industry to do without female labour. Although at first the number of women in employment fell, by 1939 37 per cent of women were in work. This was exactly the same proportion as in 1928, before the Great Depression.

?

1. In what ways did the Nazi government try to give the German people a good impression of their rule?
2. What effect did Speer in source J say the propaganda had on Germany?
3. a. What social change did Hitler claim he had achieved? (Source L.)
   b. What evidence did he put forward in support of his claim?
   c. From your knowledge of Nazi Germany, do you find his claim convincing? Explain your answer.
4. Are sources K and M more useful to historians as evidence of life under Hitler or of Nazi propaganda methods? Explain your answer.
5. What status did women have in Nazi Germany?

15

YOUNG GERMANY

● *National Socialist Youth Movements*

Hitler wanted all German children to grow up to be Nazis. They were to believe what Nazis believed. They were to be strong and fit so that boys could grow into soldiers and girls into mothers of the 'master race'. So they set up organisations to train the children.

A We start our work when the child is three. As soon as it begins to think, a little flag is put into its hand. Then comes school, the Hitler Youth Movement, the Storm Troop. We never let a single soul go.

Dr Robert Ley, a Nazi leader.

B A young child stands to attention for his Führer.

At six years old, boys joined the 'Little Fellows'. They dressed in uniforms and wore swastika armbands. Before moving up to the 'Young Folk' when they were ten, the boys had to be able to march, make maps, find direction by the stars and shoot at targets.

When they were fourteen, the boys went into the Hitler Youth itself. They went camping and played sports. They also practised marching, sang Nazi songs and learned to be loyal to Hitler. As part of their training they were taught to use weapons.

There were also girls' branches of the Hitler Youth. Between ten and fourteen years old girls could join the Young Girls' League, and at fifteen they moved up to the League of German Girls. They, too, were able to take part in exciting outdoor activities.

C 'We want to Win.' Cover of a magazine of the League of German Girls, March 1939.

Here was the chance of adventure for one twelve year old in 1938.

D I was . . . not thinking of the Führer . . . when I raised my right hand, but of . . . games, sports, hiking, singing, camping and other exciting activities . . . A uniform, a badge, an oath, a salute. There seemed to be nothing to it.

Marianne Mackinnon, The Naked Years, *1987.*

At first, no-one *had* to join the Hitler Youth. Many children still belonged to church groups or other organisations. Soon, like the political parties, all other youth organisations were banned, or became part of the Hitler Youth. After 1936 children were put under pressure to join, and in 1939 it became compulsory. The Hitler Youth had become part of 'national service'.

?

1 How does Dr Ley (source A) say that the Nazis tried to make sure that young Germans grew up to be Nazis?

2 Copy and complete these sentences, using the text and source B to help you.
In Nazi youth movements, children practised to become soldiers by

a) wearing ________________ .

b) learning ________________ .

c) learning ________________ .

d) learning ________________ .

3 In what way do sources C and D agree about what girls liked in the League of German Girls?

*E*DUCATION

Most young Germans became aware of National Socialism at school. Their teachers had to join the National Socialist Teachers' League. Lessons were to start and finish by giving the Nazi salute and saying '*Heil Hitler*!' Staff and pupils who met in the corridor were supposed to greet each other in the same way. National loyalty was encouraged by decorating schools with party symbols and teaching Nazi songs. Hitler was clear about the main duty of schools.

E Education . . . is to be the preparation for the later army service . . . The state must throw the whole weight of its educational machinery, not into pumping its children full of knowledge, but in producing absolutely healthy bodies.

Adolf Hitler, Mein Kampf.

Hitler also wanted schools to teach his racist and nationalist beliefs. To achieve his purposes, timetables gave more time to physical education, especially competitive events. Courses and textbooks were re-written to teach Nazi ideology through lessons in biology (see source F, chapter 13, p.60), German language, geography and even mathematics.

G A mentally handicapped person costs the public 4 Reichsmarks per day . . . Cautious estimates state that within the boundaries of the German Reich, 300,000 persons are being cared for in public mental institutions. How many marriage loans at 1,000 Reichsmarks per couple could annually be financed from the funds allocated to institutions?

Question from a mathematics textbook.

History lessons put across the nationalist message as pupils learned about Jewish 'crimes', the rise of National Socialism and Germany's soldier heroes. The emphasis on military glory fitted with the children's experience in the Hitler Youth.

*C*OMPULSION

Though many children were attracted by the exciting activities of the Hitler Youth, others wanted to remain members of other youth groups, like the Scouts or the Catholic Youth Club, which was strong in Bavaria. Those who resisted the pressure to join were bullied, even by the teachers. As early as 1933 members of other organisations received threatening letters.

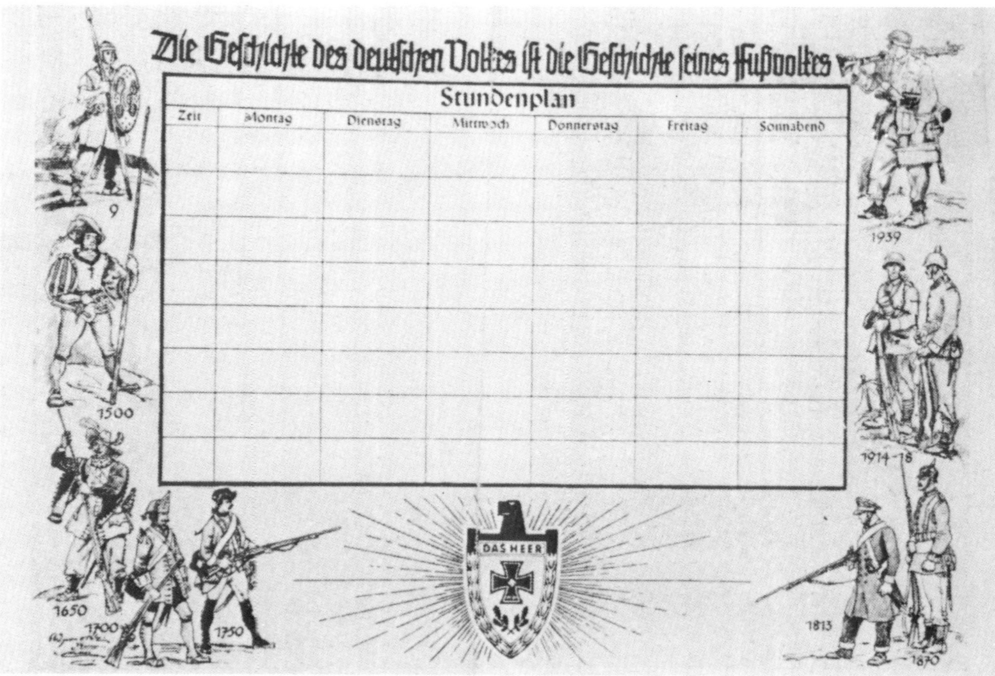

F A school timetable reflects the military ideal. The heading says 'The history of the German people is the history of its infantry'.

H The Hitler Youth comes to you today with the question: why are you still outside its ranks? We take it that you accept our Führer, Adolf Hitler. But you can only do this if you also accept the Hitler Youth created by him. If you are not willing to join the Hitler Youth then write to us on the enclosed blank.

Letter from Hitler Youth leader, Baldur von Schirach, to members of other organisations in Wiesbaden, 1933. The blank was a form which father and son had to sign, saying where they worked.

This kind of implied threat was followed by making 'youth service' compulsory by 1939.

YOUTH ACTIVITIES

Many did not need to be forced. The Hitler Youth offered action, recognition through promotion, feelings of achievement and a sense of belonging.

I Hitler Youth members on parade.

J Almost everything took the form of competitions. Not only were there contests for the best performances in sport and at work, but each unit wanted to have the best-kept home, the most interesting travel album, the top collection for the Winter Relief Fund.

Memoirs of Melita Maschmann.

Such artificial excitement did not always last. The girl who had been so pleased to join (source D) lost her enthusiasm when faced with political lectures, endless marching drills, and a discipline intended to make everyone the same.

K I felt bored with a movement which . . . expected its members to venerate [worship] a flag as if it were God Almighty, and which made me march or stand . . . for hours, listen to tiresome or inflammatory speeches . . . or shout . . . slogans which, somehow, went into one ear and out the other.

Marianne Mackinnon, The Naked Years, *1987.*

?

1. What attitude towards education did Hitler express in source E? In what ways was this attitude reflected in schools in Nazi Germany?
2. What evidence is there in sources F and G that Nazi ideas affected school lessons? Which Nazi ideals do these sources illustrate?

Imaginative reconstruction

With your group, use the sources and information in this chapter to make lists of the a) attractive b) unattractive features of Nazi youth movements. Now write a short play script in which young Germans discuss the Hitler Youth. There should be three characters:

- someone who is not a member of the movement
- a vigorous supporter who tries to convince the first person to join
- a member who has lost her/his enthusiasm and advises against joining.

The play could be performed for the class as an introduction to a discussion on the impact of Nazi youth movements.

16 OPPOSITION TO HITLER

The Working Classes

Before Hitler came to power, the Socialists and Communists had been his main opponents. Their organisations, the *Reichsbanner* and the Red Front, had fought street battles against the S.A. Surely they could be a focus of resistance?

It was not as easy as that. Following the Reichstag fire in 1933, many Communists had been imprisoned (see chapter 11). The Nazis took all the working-class movements by surprise, so quickly did they act. The main political parties were banned, trade unions made illegal, and working-men's clubs shut down. When some groups went underground, systematic raids took place on working-class districts, using the S.A., the S.S. and the Gestapo, as well as the police.

A These planned raids, together with threats, insults, beatings and arbitrary arrests . . . created an atmosphere of insecurity and helplessness even in working-class strongholds that had until recently seemed to be so safe.

Detlev Peukert, Inside Nazi Germany, *1987.*

Very quickly, even traditional working-class areas were showing their loyalty to the regime, with swastika flags flying from almost every window.

Such organised working-class resistance as did exist took two forms. The Social Democratic Party leaders who escaped arrest by fleeing abroad had information smuggled out to them about life in Germany. These, printed on green paper, were published as the 'green reports', to publicise to the world what was happening. Meanwhile, inside Germany, underground resistance groups cautiously kept in contact with each other to keep their political beliefs alive. They could do little more in the face of the terror inflicted by the Gestapo.

In 1938 one workman wrote in despair about the problem of resistance.

B Solidarity is growing, but the organisation of fighting groups on anything like a large scale is not yet possible, since the danger of being discovered is still too great.

Hitler calls this LIVING! by a member of the German Freedom Party.

Individuals

Though it was almost impossible to fight Nazism openly, the largest resistance still came from working-class people. This could be as simple as complaining about jobs, food supplies or the cost of living. As early as 1934 Gestapo reports warned about 'grumbling' over issues like food prices, which might grow into revolt.

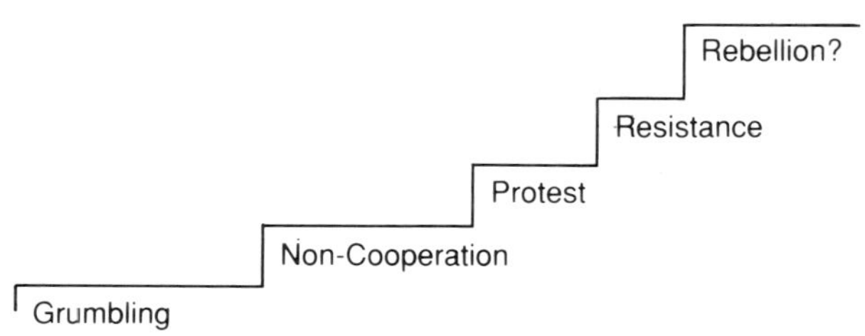

C The Stairway of Opposition.

D A typical 'wild' group from Cologne.

Some went a stage further, refusing to co-operate. Perhaps they did not send their children to the Hitler Youth, or failed to meet production targets at work. Only a few had the nerve to protest, by printing and circulating leaflets, for example, and most of these did not remain free for long.

● *Edelweiss Pirates*

In the late 1930s, some young people who did not like the military discipline of the Hitler Youth, began to meet in groups. Nicknamed 'Edelweiss Pirates' because they often wore metal edelweiss flowers on their collars, they were really local gangs.

Their main activities were at weekends. They went on camping or hiking trips, sang songs together and simply enjoyed each other's company. Like the hippies of later generations, they wanted freedom from control by authority.

These 'wild' groups saw the Hitler Youth as their enemy, and took every opportunity to beat up their patrols. They were not a serious problem for the government, but they were certainly a nuisance.

?

1. Explain why working-class movements were unable to mount effective opposition to the Nazi government.
2. How well do sources A and B agree about working-class resistance in Germany?
3. In what ways did a) ordinary Germans b) young people express their disapproval of life under the Nazis?

*T*HE CHRISTIAN CHURCHES

Co-operation

Like Socialists, Christians in Nazi Germany faced a difficult time. Many of them shared the Nazi belief in restoring German strength, but soon realised that their leaders' policies were against Christian teaching.

Hitler could not attack the churches too quickly. At first he appeared to encourage them by talking of the importance of moral values. In 1933 he agreed to guarantee the rights of the Roman Catholic Church. In return the Church promised that its priests would keep out of politics.

To control Protestants, Hitler had Ludwig Müller, a sympathiser, made Bishop of the Reich. Under him, the 'German Christians' of the Reich Church, would co-operate with the Nazis.

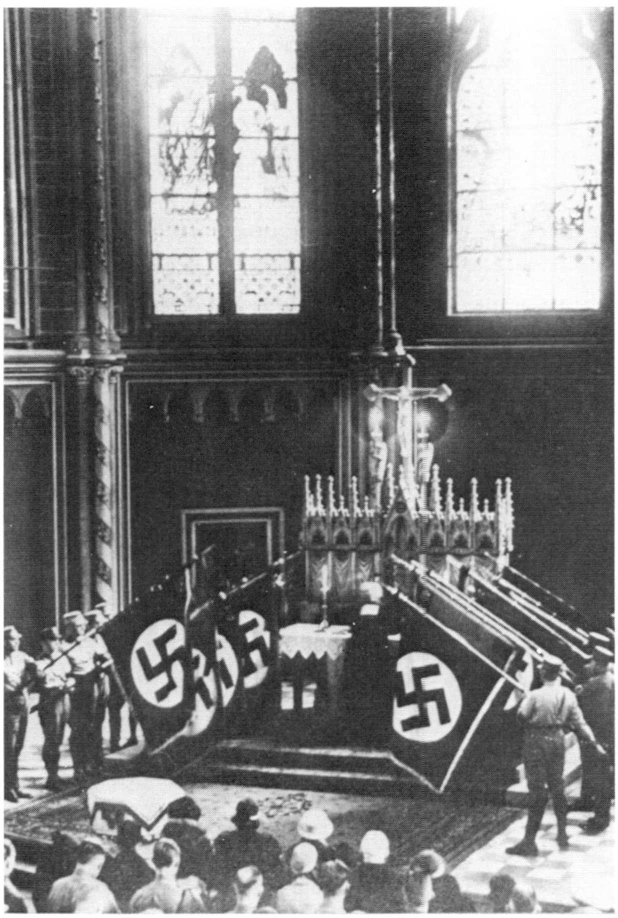

D A Nazi funeral in a Protestant Church, 1934.

Opposition

Despite these agreements, the Nazis sacked Roman Catholic civil servants and tried to shut down their youth organisations and schools. When priests or people complained, they were attacked. Many priests and monks were arrested. In 1937 the Pope issued a statement to be read in churches in Germany. In it he spoke of a 'war of destruction' against the Church, and urged Roman Catholics to oppose any actions which were against Christian beliefs.

Some Protestant pastors also stood up to the Nazis. In 1934 a former U-boat captain, Martin Niemöller, helped to found the Confessional Church. Members of this church criticised Müller's Reich Church for distorting Christian teaching. Of course, this brought them up against the Gestapo, and many pastors were arrested. Martin Niemöller himself was arrested in 1937, and was held in a concentration camp from 1938 until 1945.

Hitler made it clear that he would not take opposition, even in the name of God.

E The National Socialist State will ruthlessly make clear to those clergy who instead of being God's ministers regard it as their mission to speak insultingly of our Reich . . . that clergy . . . will be called to account before the Law like any other German citizen . . . Tens of thousands of clergy . . . fulfil their ecclesiastical duties . . . without ever coming into conflict with the laws of the State. The State considers their protection its task. The destruction of the enemies of the State is its duty.

Speech by Hitler to the Reichstag, January 1939.

F A Roman Catholic hall after an attack by the S.A. in 1933.

G A Roman Catholic priest shows his acceptance of National Socialism as he returns the salute at a parade of S.A. members in 1933.

Church resistance to the Nazis was mostly the work of brave individuals, not of proper organisations. Most church members stayed quiet, even loyal to the government, though Nazis were committing terrible acts of cruelty. Historians have sometimes criticised the churches for failing to speak clearly enough against Nazism, especially over the treatment of the Jews.

H The purpose of the church opposition was self-defence, not a wider, political opposition: the Churches, including the opponents of Nazi policies, frequently affirmed their loyalty to the state and the Führer.

The historian J.R.C. Wright.

The self-defence was necessary. During the war Hitler replaced the Bible and the Cross in German churches with *Mein Kampf* and a sword. As Professor Fritz Stern wrote, 'If Hitler had won the war, he would have attempted to destroy . . . Christianity'.

?

1 In what ways did the Nazis try to control and use the Christian churches?

2 Why are sources D and G useful as evidence of the Nazis' relationship with some Christians?

3 Why could sources E and F be seen as evidence that the Nazis were afraid of the churches?

4 What attitude does Wright in source H say the churches had towards Nazi rule?

5 What resistance did Christians make to Nazi rule?

Debate

Despite opposition from Socialists, Christians and some ordinary Germans, most Germans were loyal to Hitler, at least in public. There was little organised resistance until Germany suffered the effects of a long, hard war. Why?

Preparation

In your group gather evidence to support **one** of the following statements:
There was little open opposition to Nazi rule because

- most Germans agreed with the Nazis
- the Nazis ruled Germany well
- the Nazis' use of repression made resistance impossible
- the German people were too cowardly to resist.

Write a speech to support the statement you have chosen, lasting not more than three minutes.

Debate

One person from each group reads the speech to the class, who take notes of the main points to use later. After all groups have spoken, members of the class speak to support their group's statement or to challenge those of other groups. All points must be supported by evidence, so do not use up **all** of your evidence in your speech. After everyone has had a chance to speak, a class vote may be taken on what was the most important reason for the lack of resistance. You may not vote for your own statement.

17 THE ROAD TO WAR

In *Mein Kampf* and the Nazi Party programme of 1920, Hitler had given notice of his intentions in domestic policy. The same was true in foreign affairs. His efforts to make Germany strong again had two purposes: to overturn the Treaty of Versailles and to gain *Lebensraum* (living space) for Germany in eastern Europe. If it took war to achieve this, Hitler was willing to risk it.

He was helped in his ambitions by the policy of 'appeasement' adopted by Britain and France (see chapter 3). They felt that Germany had fair complaints about the Treaty of Versailles, and that these ought to be removed. Then Hitler would behave like a normal leader.

PREPARATIONS

Hitler gave warning of his Germany's approach to foreign policy when he withdrew from a disarmament conference in October 1933, protesting that Germany was being treated as a second-class nation. At the same time Germany left the League of Nations.

Over the next two years, the Nazis defied the military clauses of the Versailles Treaty by starting to build up their forces. Secretly, they began to build aircraft, and Hitler ordered expansion of the army and navy. In March 1935 he declared officially that Germany would no longer be bound by these clauses.

On 7 March 1936 Hitler took his first big gamble. His army marched across the Rhine to re-occupy the territory demilitarised at Versailles. Hitler waited nervously for international reaction.

A If the French had then marched into the Rhineland we would have had to withdraw with our tails between our legs, for the military resources at our disposal would have been wholly inadequate for even a moderate resistance.

Adolf Hitler, after the German re-occupation of the Rhineland.

Britain and France protested, but took no action. Hitler had got away with it.

AGGRESSION

Over the next three years Hitler set himself a series of targets. To obtain each one, he created a crisis within his target country, made demands and threats to increase tension, and prepared for war in the hope that it would not be needed.

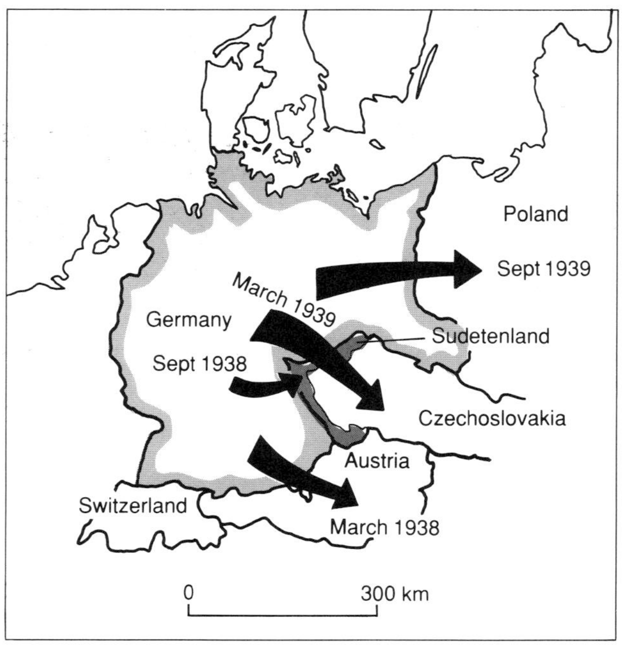

B Hitler's targets.

● *Anschluss*

The first target was the country of Hitler's birth, Austria. Nazis in Austria campaigned for Anschluss (union) between Austria and Germany. In March 1938, by threatening invasion, Hitler bullied the Austrian President into appointing a Nazi as Chancellor. Germany at once occupied Austria, the soldiers being greeted by huge demonstrations of support. The other powers did nothing, and Hitler's confidence grew.

● *Invasion of Czechoslovakia*

Almost at once, the German minority in the Sudetenland began to complain they were being mistreated by their Czech rulers. Hitler first demanded 'justice' for the Germans, then that the Sudetenland should be joined to Germany. Desperate to avoid war, the British Prime Minister Neville Chamberlain and the French Prime Minister Edouard Daladier flew to meet Hitler at Münich. Without even consulting the Czechs, they agreed that Germany could have the Sudetenland in return for a promise not to attack the rest of Czechoslovakia. They believed the peace of Europe had been saved.

Many British people feared the *Luftwaffe* would destroy their cities in a war. They greeted Chamberlain as a hero on his return.

D The Prime Minister did a noble thing in flying to Germany. Even if it did nothing else it showed the world that Great Britain is striving for peace. Every country in the world applauded his action.

Essay by Theresa Gregory, a Scottish school girl, 19 September 1938.

On 15 March 1939 German troops suddenly occupied the rest of Czechoslovakia. Appeasement had been shown to be worthless.

WHAT'S CZECHOSLOVAKIA TO ME, ANYWAY ? M

C Cartoon by the British cartoonist David Low.

Attack on Poland

When Hitler turned his attention to Poland, accusing the Poles of mistreating Germans in the 'Polish Corridor' and demanding the return of the port of Danzig, Britain and France announced they would go to war if Germany attacked Poland. They also tried to negotiate an alliance with the Soviet Union against Germany, but were horrified when the Russians signed an agreement with the Germans instead.

After their previous weakness, Hitler thought the Western powers would not live up to their promise to defend Poland. On 1 September his forces launched a blitzkrieg on Poland. This time his calculations were wrong. Two days later, after an ultimatum requiring him to withdraw, Britain and France declared war. Adolf Hitler had taken Germany into a second World War.

?

1. Describe in your own words
   - Hitler's aims in foreign policy
   - the policy of Britain and France towards Germany.
2. What evidence is there in source A that Hitler was not sure of being successful in re-occupying the Rhineland?
3. Look back at source F, chapter 3. In what way could Hitler try to justify his claims on Austria, Czechoslovakia and Poland? Do you find such arguments convincing? Explain your answer.
4. Do sources C and D agree about the British and French policy of appeasement? Explain your answer.
5. What arguments could be used for and against the policy of appeasement?

INDEX